GARLAND STUDIES IN

THE HISTORY OF AMERICAN LABOR

edited by
STUART BRUCHEY
ALLAN NEVINS PROFESSOR EMERITUS
COLUMBIA UNIVERSITY

RACE, SPACE AND YOUTH LABOR MARKETS

MICHAEL A. STOLL

Routledge
Taylor & Francis Group
LONDON AND NEW YORK

First published 1999 by Garland Publishing, Inc.

Published 2018 by Routledge
2 Park Square, Milton Park, Abingdon, Oxon OX14 4RN
52 Vanderbilt Avenue, New York, NY 10017

First issued in paperback 2018

Routledge is an imprint of the Taylor & Francis Group, an informa business

Copyright © 1999 by Michael A. Stoll

All rights reserved. No part of this book may be reprinted or reproduced or utilised in any form or by any electronic, mechanical, or other means, now known or hereafter invented, including photocopying and recording, or in any information storage or retrieval system, without permission in writing from the publishers.

Notice:
Product or corporate names may be trademarks or registered trademarks, and are used only for identification and explanation without intent to infringe.

Library of Congress Cataloging-in-Publication Data

Stoll, Michael A.
    Race, space and youth labor markets / Michael A. Stoll.
    p.   cm. — (Garland studies in the history of American labor)
    Includes bibliographical references and index.
    ISBN 0-8153-3306-4 (alk. paper)
    1. Youth—Employment—United States. 2. Labor market—United States. 3. Minorities—Employment—United States. 4. Metropolitan areas—United States. 5. Urban economics. 6. Sociology, Urban—United States. I. Title. II. Series.
HD6273.S76 1999
331.3'4'0973—dc21

                                                98-55172

ISBN 13: 978-1-138-88020-7 (pbk)
ISBN 13: 978-0-8153-3306-7 (hbk)

For my parents and grandmothers

Contents

List of Tables	ix
Preface	xiii
Acknowledgments	xvii
Chapter 1 Introduction	3
Chapter 2 The Spatial Mismatch hypothesis Revisited	13
Kain's Formulation of the Problem	14
Is Race a Factor in Urban Labor Markets?	17
Is Space a Barrier to Black and Latino Employment?	22
Spatial Mismatch in the Youth Labor Market	37
Conclusion	40
Chapter 3 Does Living in the Suburbs Really Make a Difference? Residential Location and the Dynamic Labor Market Outcomes of Young Males	43
Joblessness in Central Cities and Suburbs	45
Dimensions of Joblessness in Central Cities and Suburbs	47
Concentration and Distribution of Jobless Spells Across Residential Areas	54
Conclusion	63
Chapter 4 The Impact of Job Movement from Central Cities to Suburbs on Young Men's Employment	65
Metropolitan Distribution of Jobs and People and Dimensions of Young Men's Joblessness	66
Data, Empirical Model, and Definitions of Variables	69
Results of Jobless Duration Models	72

Conclusion	86
Chapter 5 The Confounding Influence of Race in Space: The Effect of Race and Residential Location on the Employment of Young Men in the Washington, DC Area	93
The Dynamics of Black Suburbanization	95
The Washington, DC Setting	97
The Analysis	100
Conclusion	130
Chapter 6 The Case for Preserving Targeted Policy Approaches to Ease the Employment Difficulties of Minority Youth	135
Space or Race?	135
When Might Race Matter?	137
Universal or Targeted Policies?	139
The Appropriate Policy Mix	142
Appendices	153
References	165
Notes	177
Index	185

List of Tables

Chapter 1

Table 1.1	Employment-to-Population Ratios and Unemployment Rates for 16 to 24-Year-Olds by Race and Sex	11

Chapter 2

Table 2.1	Median Male Earnings, Unemployment, and Occupational Status by Race and Residential Location for 12 Largest SMSAs in 1965 or 1966	23
Table 2.2	Mean Travel Times, Employment Rates, and the Share of Racial Employment Gap Explained by Predicted Travel Time Differences in 1980: Logit Models	34

Chapter 3

Table 3.1	Unemployment and Jobless Rates by Race and Residential Location: 1984	46
Table 3.2	Dimensions of Unemployment by Race and Residential Location: 1984	49
Table 3.3	Mean Weeks Unemployment and Jobless Duration by Race and Residential Location: 1984	51
Table 3.4	Proportion of Unemployment and Jobless Spells Ending Within One Month by Race and Residential Location: 1984	55
Table 3.5	Proportion of Unemployment by Race and Residential Location: 1984	577

Table 3.6	Likelihood of Unemployment Spells Ending in Employment/Withdrawal by Race and Residential Location: 1984	59
Table 3.7	Distribution of Unemployment and Joblessness by Race and Residential Location: 1984	61
Chapter 4		
Table 4.1	Percentage of Jobs and Population in Central Cities of US Metropolitan Areas, 1970–1990	67
Table 4.2	Dimensions of Young Males' (Aged 19 to 27) Unemployment by Race: 1984	68
Table 4.3	Definition of Variables	71
Table 4.4	Means (std. dev.) for White, Black, and Latino Central City Models	73
Table 4.5	Maximum Likelihood Weibull Estimates of Jobless Durations for Central City Young Males	74
Table 4.6	Means (std. dev.) for White, Black, and Latino Suburban Models	82
Table 4.7	Maximum Likelihood Weibull Estimates of Jobless Durations for Suburban Young Males	83
Chapter 5		
Table 5.1	Prince George's County, MD, and Washington, DC Population by Race from 1970 to 1990	98
Table 5.2	Change in Jobs, Employees, and Job Import Ratios in Washington, DC and Prince George's County, MD, from 1970 to 1990	99
Table 5.3	Labor Market Outcomes for Males Aged 16–21 and Washington, DC Concentration of Racial Groups Across the Washington, DC and Prince George's County, MD Area: 1990	101
Table 5.4	Comparisons of Young Men's (Aged 16 to 21) Labor Market Outcomes in Washington, DC and Prince George's County, MD by Race, School Enrollment Status and Education: 1990	102
Table 5.5	Comparisons of Black/White and Latino/White Labor Market Outcome Ratios for Males Aged 16–21 in Washington, DC and Prince George's County, MD by School Enrollment Status and Education: 1990	106
Table 5.6	Definition of Variables	109

List of Tables

Table 5.7	Personal and Family Background Means for Employed and Jobless by Race and Residential Location: 1990	110
Table 5.8	Means (std. dev.) for Residential Location Equations	112
Table 5.9	Pooled Employment Equations Across Residential Location for Young White, Black, and Latino Males	114
Table 5.10	Decomposition of Black-White Racial Employment Rate Difference	122
Table 5.11	Decomposition of Latino-White Ethnic Employment Rate Difference	123
Table 5.12	Contribution of Prince George's Residential Location to Racial Employment Rate Differentials	124

Preface

The purpose of this book is to examine whether physical distance from jobs or racial discrimination in youth labor markets explains a greater part of minority youth's employment problems. The study of youth labor markets is not new. After scholars uncovered a growing gap between the unemployment levels of youth and adults during the 1960s and 1970s, a number of articles and books began to emerge that attempted to identify those factors negatively affecting youth's employment. What instead emerged from this analysis was the observation of a large and growing racial gap in employment within the youth labor market itself. While youth in general performed badly in relation to adults in labor markets, it was found that minority youth's jobless levels were significantly higher than those of their white counterparts.

Minority youth's employment problems were not always more intractable than those of their white counterparts. In the 1940s and 1950s, black youth employment levels were fairly high and stable, relative to those that we observe today, and much more aligned with those of their white counterparts. This was true because in those years black youth still tended to live in the Southern region of the United States and worked in agricultural industries where employment was steady, but at extremely low pay. After the second great migration of blacks from the South into Northern and Western parts of the United States in the 1940s and 1950s, and after the children of the first wave of migrants out of the South grew into their teenage years, the jobless problems of black youth exploded to the unacceptable levels that we witness today.

A host of explanations emerged to explain the low employment levels of minority youth. These included the weak skill levels of black youth, the differential methods that black and white youth use to get a job, racial discrimination in hiring against black youth, lack of employment opportunities for youth in general, the high reservation wages of black youth, increased competition for jobs by other groups such as women and the characteristics of jobs available for black youth, among many other factors. Much of this earlier work had a profound impact in government circles, particularly during the 1970s, on the thinking of the youth employment problem and on the variety of ways to design policy intervention. Indeed, what emerged during this time was a significant federal government response to solve the youth, and particularly the minority youth, employment problem. Large federal funds were earmarked to such programs and acts as Job Corps and the Youth Employment and Demonstration Project Act of 1977, respectively, to ease the employment problems of youth. However, such efforts were not sustained over time, thus allowing youth employment problems to go unsolved and racial differences in youth employment to persist.

In recent years, there has been a growing concern by academics and policy-makers that the continuing problem of minority employment, especially in the case of youth, is related to structural changes in the economy that have manifested themselves geographically. Urban sprawl continues at an unprecedented pace, with metropolitan areas becoming much more suburbanized than ever before. The consequence of this trend is that new companies, and therefore new jobs, continue to locate in the suburban periphery far from central city areas where original city development began. However, what makes these trends troubling is the continuing observation of racial discrimination in housing markets, particularly as expressed in suburbs, which, by and large, has had the result of restricting blacks' housing options to the central city parts of metropolitan areas. Needless to say, such geographically based patterns are likely to undermine blacks' access to jobs.

This book tackles the question of space in youth labor markets and also examines whether and how race may act to limit black youth's access to jobs. Blacks' continue to make strides in educational attainment, particularly in the receipt of a high school diploma, both absolutely and relative to whites. However, their employment rate has remained at least twice that of their white counterparts for nearly two

Preface

decades. Naturally, such trends leads one to wonder whether black youth are treated differently in the labor market than similar white youth. Moreover, the extent to which differential treatment of blacks is much more severe and pronounced in the suburban than in the central city labor market has a particularly strong impact on the extent to which we believe geography matters in the employment of minority youth. It is these issued that are pursued in this book.

Two central questions guide this analysis: Does the spatial mismatch between the locations of jobs in which youth are traditionally employed and youth's residences explain young black and Latino males' worse labor market outcomes in relation to those of whites in metropolitan areas? And, what is the relative importance, and their possible interactions, of spatial mismatch and race, or how minority youth are treated in labor markets, in determining young blacks' and Latinos' worse labor market outcomes? In the introduction of this book, I lay out this conceptual problem in more detail. The remainder of this book serves as a test of this "spatial mismatch" and racial discrimination hypotheses. In chapter 2, I critically review the major works related to the spatial mismatch hypothesis, and attempt to show, theoretically, how race can confound space in these studies. In chapter 3, the spatial mismatch hypothesis is tested by comparing the employment outcomes of young males living in the central cities and suburbs using dynamic measures of unemployment. In chapter 4, I analyze the impact of the movement of jobs from central cities to suburbs on young males employment outcomes and examine how the racial makeup of central cities and suburbs may influence the hiring of racial minorities. In chapter 5, I use the case of black suburbanization in the Washington, DC area to explore the relative importance of race and space and how they might interact to cause lower black youth employment. Finally, in the conclusion, I discuss the policy implications of this study.

M.A.S.
Los Angeles, CA
September, 1998

Acknowledgments

Identifying and giving proper respects to those who assisted in this endeavor might just be as difficult as writing the book itself! So many people, in some way, shape, or form, have contributed to this work. I may not remember all those who gave even the littlest bit of information and time, but I will certainly try my best. To those who contributed, but whose name does not appear here, I apologize and mean no harm by the omittance.

First and foremost, I am truly indebted to Frank Levy, Edwin Melendez, and Paul Osterman. To Frank, I have benefited immensely from your sharp intellect and ability to identify problems and suggest solutions. I have also learned from you that, though much more difficult, a product becomes much better when one improves on a technique or idea rather than repeating what others have done. To Edwin, you have never allowed me to rest on any laurels. You have always showed me what it means and takes to pursue excellence. I have grown tremendously under your guidance and I hope that our relationship can continue to bloom as it has the past six years. To Paul, from you I have learned how to look at the "big" picture. It is so easy to get lost in the details. But from your constructive feedback, I have learned how to retreat from the work in order to get a fresh and new perspective. Thank you all for being there for me.

I could not have finished this book without data acquisition and technical assistance. I thank Steve McClaskie of Ohio State University for his help in acquiring and answering questions about the National Longitudinal Survey of Youth (NLSY). Similarly, I thank Mallory Stark at MIT and Roy Williams at the Massachusetts Institute of Social and Economic Research (University of Massachusetts-Amherst) for their help in my acquiring the 1990 US Census Public Use Microdata Samples. Gourish Hosangady of the University of Massachusetts, Boston, and Art Anjer at MIT were very instrumental in the beginning programming and formatting stage of the data analysis. Jay Mangalvedhe at the Maryland-National Capital Park and Planning Commission must be thanked for his assistance in answering questions and providing data on Prince George's County, MD, during my case study of the Washington, DC area.

I also benefited greatly from administrative support during this project. The staff at the Gaston Institute, University of Massachusetts, Boston, was extremely generous in providing me with computer and office resources during the entire book writing process. To them, I am grateful. Also, I must thank Williams College for the resident fellowship given to me that freed up my time so that I could write the bulk of the analysis. While at Williams College, I received tremendous support from the college administrative staff and the staff at the Department of Economics. Danielle Deane at Williams College provided final editorial corrections. I thank her for her work. At MIT, Sandy Welford and Rolf Engler were tremendously helpful and resourceful. Also, Isaac Colbert and Margo Daniels Tyler in the Dean's Office at MIT were tremendously supportive of my work and provided me with useful advice.

I also received a considerable amount of intellectual, emotional, and financial support that allowed me to complete this study. I must thank the Social Science Research Council's Program on the Urban Underclass for a fellowship that allowed me to begin the groundwork of this study, and I must thank the Economic Policy Institute for their fellowship which covered the bulk of the research costs. I also benefited from a grant from the U.S. Department of Housing and Urban Development. During my stay at Williams College, the faculty in the Department of Economics at Williams College were very helpful in providing comments, criticisms and suggestions of early drafts of various chapters. I benefited greatly and learned a tremendous amount about academic life during my year at Williams College. Others, such as Phil Clay at MIT, Boyd James at Drew University, and Kaye Husbands at Williams College, provided guidance and mentoring during this book writing process. I have grown tremendously from their advice and their willingness to participate in my development.

Various parts of this book have been originally published in journals. Much of the discussion on spatial mismatch and racial

Acknowledgments

discrimination in chapter 2 of this book was published in *Sage Race Relations*, vol. 21(4), 1996, pp. 3–25, as "Distance or Discrimination? The Convergence of Race and Space in Understanding Metropolitan Racial Differences in Employment." Also, Tables 1 and 2 in chapter 4 of this book were originally published by *Urban Studies*, vol. 35(12), 1998, as "When Jobs Move, Do Black and Latino Men Lose: The Effect of Growth in Job Decentralization on Young Men's Jobless Duration and Incidence." I thank these journals for allowing me to reprint some of this work.

Finally, it is with great feeling that I thank my family and close friends for giving me love and support during the writing period of this book. To my lovingly companion and friend, Nahn, I thank you with all my heart for your support and understanding. I gain and learn tremendously from your inner-strength and inner-peace.

The work that provided the basis for this publication was supported by funding under a grant from the U.S. Department of Housing and Urban Development. The substance and findings of that work are dedicated to the public. The author and publisher are solely responsible for the accuracy of the statements and interpretations contained in the publication. Such interpretations do not necessarily reflect the views of the U.S. Government.

Race, Space and Youth Labor Markets

CHAPTER 1
Introduction

Over the past three decades, joblessness among young people in the U.S. has always been particularly high, especially when viewed against the employment levels of adults. Some might say that we need not be concerned about youth's employment problems because it seems reasonable to expect that young people will perform worse in the labor market than their adult counterparts. After all, young people, more often than not, are unsure about what they want to do in life, and spend much of their youth in school or working in different jobs and industries trying to figure out their occupational niche in life. Over time, however, as young people begin to settle down, exit school and age in the labor market and given their multitude of experiences with different jobs, they eventually choose an occupational path, thereby stabilizing their employment trajectories and minimizing their jobless experiences. Seen in this light, young people's employment problems should not be viewed with any particular concern because their joblessness is only a temporary state, simply a function of their uncertainty about what they want to do in life.

If this dynamic were true of all youth, perhaps we need not be concerned about the high jobless rates of youth, particularly those who are out-of-school and possess limited education. High joblessness among this group would simply be viewed as an inevitable consequence of being young, with no long term negative consequences on future labor market performance. However, if indeed there are some youth whose joblessness is extremely high and persists over time relative to other youth groups, we may need be concerned because such persistent joblessness may tend to produce scarring effects over time. This is to say that if youth are unable to develop on-the-job skills and work experience while on a job precisely because they unable to attain or maintain employment, they may be more likely than others to experience relatively lower wages and higher unemployment as they age in the labor market (Osterman 1978; Stevenson 1978). Such is the situation of black, and to a large extent Latino, youth in the U.S. Over the past two and a half decades, comparisons of employment outcomes among black, Latino and white youth invariably show the extent to which black and Latino youth fall considerably behind their white counterparts in obtaining employment. Black and Latino youth's unemployment rates have consistently been at least one-and-a-half to three times as high as that of their white youth counterparts since the 1960s. High levels of joblessness among black and Latino youth, then, are a major social problem worthy of policy consideration not only because of the problems inherent in not having a job at any particular time, but also because such persistent joblessness among minority youth is likely to cause future labor market problems thus allowing racial inequalities to endure.

Relevant policies to combat persistent minority youth joblessness, however, cannot be designed without knowing its causes.[1] Many explanations of minority joblessness have been proposed, generally falling under supply-side and demand-side categories. Supply-side explanations include those factors over which youth themselves may control, such as the investment decision to stay in school, and their attitudes and willingness to work. The most prominent of these supply-side explanations include the high reservation wages of black youth (Holzer 1986; Anderson 1980), the lack of work ethic of black youth due to cultural traits (Sowell 1990), the absence of positive role models for black, inner-city youth (Wilson 1986; Datcher-Loury and Loury 1986) and the lack of relevant skills (Kasarda 1986). Moreover, language and immigration status have also been offered as supply-side explanations of Latinos' joblessness (Neidert and Tienda 1983). Demand-side explanations of minority youth joblessness include those factors over which youth themselves have little control. These include fluctuations in aggregate demand (Freeman 1990; Cain and Finnie 1990), and racial discrimination (Cherry 1988; Culp and Dunson 1986), among other reasons. In recent years, the spatial mismatch hypothesis, as proposed by Kain (1968) and revived by Kasarda (1985) and Wilson (1987), has become a dominant demand-side explanation of why black youth perform so poorly in the labor market relative to their white counterparts in metropolitan areas. According to this hypothesis, the

Introduction

twin processes of the residential segregation of blacks to the central city and the movement of jobs, particularly low-skill jobs, from the central city to the suburbs have combined to undermine black youth's physical accessibility to jobs, thereby reducing their employment opportunities in metropolitan areas.[2] In other words, blacks' employment is low both absolutely and relative to whites because blacks, unlike their white counterparts, are more likely to live in central cities where job loss has been occurring since the 1960s. In addition, blacks, unlike whites, face housing market discrimination in the suburbs which limits their ability to follow jobs there. Blacks' inability to follow jobs to the suburbs constrains their search for work to the central cities where job growth has been stagnant. The resulting oversupply of black labor relative to diminishing job opportunities in the central city drives up the black unemployment rate both absolutely and relative to whites in metropolitan areas.

This hypothesis seems an attractive explanation of high minority youth joblessness not only because of its intuitive appeal, but also because the images that it conjures up in our minds are consistent with the employment outcomes that we perceive to be true in labor markets. Blacks' employment levels are low relative to those of whites. Blacks tend to live in central cities. Thoughts of central cities tend to conjure up images of areas where housing is dilapidated and buildings are boarded up, where businesses are abandoned, thus providing few job opportunities, where crime and drug dealing run rampant, and where welfare-dependency runs deep. Whites tend to live in the suburbs. Thoughts of the suburbs, on the other hand, tend to conjure up images of newer housing, little crime or drug dealing, and freshly paved streets with huge shopping malls on open lots providing multiple job opportunities. Whether or not these images are correct is less important than the fact that they help shape our interpretation of reality.

The images of the central city are reinforced by Wilson's (1986) underclass thesis of entrenched urban poverty. To Wilson, the combination of structural changes in the economy, of which the spatial mismatch hypothesis is a major part, combined with black middle-class flight to the suburbs has left behind in central cities the black poor, socially isolated from mainstream America and vulnerable to "concentration effects" that have produced "dysfunctional" behavior. Since black youth are more likely to live in these central city areas than are white youth, it seems reasonable to conclude that they should have more jobless problems than their white counterparts.

The empirical results of spatial mismatch as an explanation of blacks' higher joblessness both absolutely and relative to whites have been mixed, however, with more recent studies tending to support this hypothesis of blacks' employment problems. Perhaps one reason why these studies have had such mixed results stems from researchers' inability to control for the role of race in labor markets, or how blacks are treated in relation to whites during the employment process. In recent discussions, the spatial mismatch hypothesis of blacks' lower employment, and the underclass thesis of black poverty for that matter, both talk about race, but they both implicitly reject its importance in the labor market as a determinant of blacks' labor market problems. The spatial mismatch hypothesis explicitly deals with the problems of race in housing markets, but neglects its importance in the labor market. Spatial mismatch studies that neglect to control for or take into account the role of race in labor markets, I contend, will tend to confound, and possibly overstate, the importance of space in the labor market, since greater racial discrimination in employment in suburbs than in central cities can also cause blacks' employment to be low both absolutely and relative to whites. That is, if employers' decisions to move out of central cities is in part reflective of their desire to distance themselves from black communities, and therefore such discriminating employers are more likely to be located in suburbs than central cities, it is difficult to say whether the resulting spatial mismatch of jobs and blacks' residential locations is purely a problem of space. Likewise, if employment discrimination against blacks is much more severe in suburban areas where jobs have moved, it is difficult to determine whether the distance of jobs from blacks' residential locations is in fact a cause of blacks' higher joblessness, or a by-product of racial discrimination in hiring. In such a situation, even if blacks were to overcome the problems of space by taking more time and spending more money to search for or commute to suburban jobs, they may be unlikely to get such jobs since suburban firms would more likely discriminate against them in hiring.

Why is a book about racial and spatial barriers to employment for minority youth important? As we shall see, the jobless rates of minority youth are disturbingly high, and this alone, I contend, makes such a book about its causes a justified endeavor. But of all the competing explanations of minority joblessness, why chose to examine and evaluate the spatial and racial explanations of race differences in youth's employment outcomes? First, I do so because along with the

Introduction

weak skills story, the spatial mismatch and the racial discrimination hypotheses are dominant explanations of minorities' employment difficulties. Second, I pursue this course of investigation because of my curiosity about race in labor markets. Although the spatial mismatch talks about race and racial differences in employment, the hypothesis, as it is currently discussed, implicitly rejects or minimizes its importance in labor markets. Third, I contend that these two hypothesis, though they at first appear to be competing explanations of minority youths' joblessness, are intimately tied together. It is very difficult to tell from results of spatial mismatch studies whether or not physical distance is the reason why blacks cannot get jobs in job-rich suburbs, or whether it is because greater racial discrimination in suburban areas limits their access to jobs there.

The last of these issues raises the question about the nature of these two hypotheses. On first glance, it appears as though the spatial mismatch hypothesis is concerned about the explaining the absolute differences of whites', blacks', and Latinos' employment in the central city versus the suburbs. That is, it seems as though support for the spatial mismatch hypothesis is achieved if any or all of these groups' employment levels are greater in the suburbs than in the central city. On the other hand, the racial discrimination hypothesis seems to be concerned about the relative differences in outcomes between these two groups irrespective of their residential location. If we believe that the spatial mismatch hypothesis is an important cause of minorities' low employment levels, policy makers might be concerned about moving blacks and Latinos to the suburbs in order to improve their employment levels absolutely. But if blacks and Latinos tend to do worse relative to whites in the suburbs than in the central city, should we be concerned and should we still take this as support for the spatial mismatch hypothesis? Or should society only be concerned with polices that increase blacks' and Latinos' employment levels absolutely by moving such groups from central cities to suburbs?

It is my contention that we should be concerned about both the absolute and relative measures of black advancement because of the principles of fairness and equal opportunity. It is not acceptable that equally qualified black or Latino youth in any residential area should have worse labor market opportunities than comparable whites. And we should not accept that raising blacks' or Latinos' employment levels absolutely is a necessary condition for progress if racial differences in employment remain even after policy intervention.

On closer inspection, however, one could argue that the spatial mismatch hypothesis is not only a hypothesis about absolute differences between suburban and central city residents labor market outcomes, but also a hypothesis that attempts to explain the relative differences between racial groups labor market outcomes in metropolitan areas. At its core, it suggests that if there was no housing market discrimination against blacks and Latinos in the suburbs, that blacks and Latinos, like whites, would be able adjust their housing location decisions by moving to suburbs in order to follow jobs, thereby either keeping the racial differences in labor market outcomes constant or reducing them in metropolitan areas. It is imperative, then, that we be concerned about both the absolute and relative differences in employment for policy purposes.

Having shed light on the reasoning behind this study, I set out to investigate three main issues. First, I critically examine the merits of the spatial mismatch hypothesis as an explanation of minority joblessness by comparing the labor market outcomes of suburban and central city residents using dynamic measures of unemployment. Most research in this area uses static labor market outcome measures. However, the unemployment rate is made up of dynamic parts. By decomposing the unemployment rate into its dynamic parts, one can determine where the biggest racial differences in unemployment are generated. Dynamic measures of unemployment, such as the number of spells or the duration of unemployment, should be examined, then, to determine which of the component parts of unemployment contribute most to racial unemployment rate differences. Once these components are determined, they should then be used in the analysis to give a more precise estimate of the factors that affect unemployment, which in turn, should provide a better understanding and a more accurate analysis of racial differences in unemployment.

Second, I attempt to assess the importance of the job decentralization (meaning the extent of job suburbanization) in metropolitan areas, as an explanation of black and Latino youth's low employment both absolutely and relative to whites. If we think, as recent research suggests, that jobs continue to move from central cities to the suburbs, and if we think that black and Latino young men are more likely to live in central cities than in suburbs compared to their white counterparts, then minority youth may be at a spatial disadvantage in the labor market as their ability to attain employment

Introduction 9

will be compromised by the extent to which jobs are suburbanized and the extent to which suburban housing market discrimination exists.

Third, I attempt to assess the relative importance of a suburban residential location and racial discrimination in labor markets, and their possible interactions, as explanations of racial employment differences. Although a suburban residential location may increase black and Latino youth's employment opportunities absolutely, thereby improving their labor market outcomes relative to their central city counterparts, racial discrimination in suburban labor markets may also limit the employment benefits that might be gained by living in them. Sorting out which of these factors is more important, and examining how they interact, should help our understanding of black and Latino youth's employment problems in metropolitan areas. This improved understanding, in turn, should also benefit us in deciding on the appropriate types of policies that we think are necessary to mitigate the employment difficulties of black and Latino youth.

In this book, I address these issues using data from the National Longitudinal Survey of Youth (NLSY) and the 1990 *U.S. Census*.[3] The data from the NLSY are drawn from metropolitan areas in the continental United States.[4] In addition, since the spatial mismatch hypothesis suggests that residential location matters in employment outcomes, I use the central city or suburban residential location as the principle measure of space.

I use 1990 *US Census* data to examine the Washington, DC area as a case-study to examine the relative importance of residential location and race as explanations of racial differences in youth employment. The Washington, DC area represents a natural experiment to investigate these issues since black suburbanization into Prince George's County, Maryland has occurred precisely where tremendous employment growth has also occurred over the last 20 years. As we will see in the next chapter, some have criticized the use of residential location as a poor measure of space because it can, to a large extent, reveal little about proximity to jobs. That is, having a suburban residence may not improve one's spatial job accessibility if one does not live near suburban job growth centers. This is particularly true in the case of blacks since they tend to move to those parts of the suburbs that are adjacent to central city minority areas and that have experienced limited job growth (Galster 1987; Kain 1985). Thus, for blacks, having a suburban residential location need not imply that they are closer to the nexus of job opportunities than their central city counterparts. The

Washington, DC case helps to sort this issue out because of the unique suburbanization patterns that have occurred there for blacks.

Before we move into the main discussion, a preliminary look at racial differences in employment seems reasonable to document and justify the study of employment problems of minority youth. Table 1.1 shows some employment outcomes by race over a twenty year period for youth aged 16–24. It is clear that the employment problems of minority youth measured in any way and in any time period are much worse than those of their white counterparts. From 1970 to 1990, young white males' employment-to-population ratio edged slightly upwards, but their unemployment rate increased as well. Unlike young white males, however, young black males' employment difficulties show a clear pattern of deterioration over time. Much of this decline in black male employment occurred during the 1970s. Young black males' employment-to-population ratio declined sharply from 1970 to 1990, while their unemployment rate ballooned from 12.4 in 1970 to 23.7 in 1990. As a consequence of these diverging employment patterns between black and white male youth, the black/white employment-to-population ratio declined markedly from .89 in 1970 to .72 in 1990, showing relative black male youth employment losses. At the same time, the black/white unemployment rate ratio increased dramatically from 1.75 in 1970 to 2.39 in 1990, showing increased employment difficulties of blacks. Like young white males, young Latino males' employment-to-population ratio rose during these two decades, but it remained lower than that of whites in each of the years. Thus, although a Latino/white employment-to-population ratio gap existed in 1990, it has narrowed over time since 1970. Young Latino males' unemployment rate has increased slightly from 1970 to 1990 and this change has contributed to the growing Latino/white unemployment rate ratio from 1980 to 1990, though it still remains lower than it did in 1970.

The racial differences for young females are slightly different than they are for males. Table 1.1 shows that young white females' employment-to-population ratio increased dramatically from 1970 to 1990, while their unemployment rate has remained fairly stable during this same period. Young black females' employment-to-population ratio has remained fairly constant, increasing slightly from .40 in 1970 to .42 in 1990. However, their unemployment rate rose sharply during this time period. Thus, although the female black/white employment-to-

Table 1.1: Employment-to-Population Ratios and Unemployment Rates for 16 to 24-Year-Olds By Race and Sex

	\multicolumn{8}{c}{Males}							
	White		Black		Latino/a		Black/White		Latino/White	
	Emp Ratios	Unemp Rate	Emp Ratios	Unemp Rate	Emp Ratios	Unemp Rate	Emp Ratios	UnempRate	Emp Ratios	UnempRate
1970	.61	7.1	.54	12.4	.52	10.3	.89	1.75	.85	1.45
1980	.67	10.6	.45	22.0	.59	13.3	.67	2.08	.88	1.25
1990	.65	9.9	.47	23.7	.60	13.4	.72	2.39	.92	1.35

	\multicolumn{10}{c}{Females}
1970	.49	6.0	.40	13.1	.36	10.4	.82	2.18	.73	1.73
1980	.58	9.4	.38	24.0	.44	12.7	.66	2.55	.76	1.35
1990	.59	7.3	.42	18.9	.43	11.7	.71	2.59	.73	1.60

Source: 1970, 1980, 1990 *US Census of Population, U.S. Summary*, and 1970 and 1980 *US Census of Population, Persons of Spanish Origin Subject Report*. Note: Employment-to-population ratios and unemployment rates were calculated for the civilian noninstitutional population.

population ratio declined from 1970 to 1990 as it did for males, it declined for a very different reason; young white females' employment-to-population ratio increased much more rapidly than it did for black females. However, like males, the female black/white unemployment rate ratio increased dramatically from 1970 to 1990, precisely for the same reason the male black/white ratio increased. Like young white and black females, young Latinas' employment-to-population ratio increased rather markedly during this period. Their unemployment rate remained fairly constant, though higher than that of young white females. Thus, the Latina/white employment-to-population ratio has remained constant over time, while the Latina/white unemployment rate ratio has declined slightly during this period.[5]

It is clear then that black youth's employment outcomes have deteriorated since 1970 and have fallen considerably in relation to their white counterparts. This deterioration in blacks' employment occurred more rapidly in the 1970s than in the 1980s. However, while black male youth's employment outcomes eroded in absolute terms during this period, those for black females did not. On the other hand, Latino youth's employment outcomes, though worse than those of whites, have not fallen relatively. The spatial mismatch hypothesis suggests that the explanation of black and white males divergent employment outcomes over time can be found in the fact that jobs have moved to the suburbs, while exclusionary housing practices there have kept blacks, but not whites, from following them. Therefore, whites were able to move to the suburbs without constraints and took advantage of job opportunities there that seemingly evaded blacks. As we shall see in chapter 4, jobs continue to move from the central cities to the suburbs, while blacks and Latinos residential locations remain in the central city. The spatial mismatch in this context seems to have a considerable amount of appeal in explaining these racial employment trends since one reason for blacks and Latinos apparent inability to decentralize and follow jobs that left for the suburbs is that their parents could not move to the suburbs because of housing market discrimination. Although space may have become a serious impediment to employment for blacks and Latinos, it is not clear whether job discrimination in both the suburbs and central city is more important than these spatial reasons. It is this conceptual puzzle that I attempt to sort out in this book.

CHAPTER 2
The Spatial Mismatch Hypothesis Revisited

There is little doubt that black, and to a lesser extent Latino, unemployment in the U.S. has been about two times the level of whites' over the past three decades. This problem is amplified in the case of youth. In this chapter, I review the major works over the past 25 years or so which have attempted to tackle issues of race, space and employment. Although the focus of this study is on young men, I do not limit the review to those works that only examine youth for two reasons. First, the impact of residential segregation and job decentralization on the labor market outcomes of adults, particularly black adults, will be amplified in the case of youth, since young adults fare so much worse in the labor market than their adult counterparts. Second, researchers use the case of youth to control for a key methodological problem in spatial mismatch research. This problem is labeled "residential enodegeneity bias," and simply refers to the inability of researchers to tell whether people who would do well in the labor market anyway are more likely to move to or live in the suburbs. If this is true, the greater employment outcomes of suburban than central city residents that we are likely to observe may just simply reflect this residential mobility bias rather than a true impact of residential location on employment. Researchers use the case of youth because they are more likely not to choose their residential location and are more likely to live at home where residential location choices are made by their parents.

KAIN'S FORMULATION OF THE PROBLEM

In 1968, John Kain published a widely cited article in which he argued that the low levels of black employment was in part attributable to an increasing number of jobs, particularly manufacturing jobs, that were moving to the suburban ring and to housing market discrimination practices that restricted blacks' residential choices to the central city. Moreover, this practice of residential segregation kept blacks from participating in the general patterns of metropolitan population decentralization, or, in other words, kept blacks from following the movement of jobs to the suburbs in the same way that whites had been able to follow them. Kain (1968), using data from Chicago and Detroit, advanced three distinct hypotheses. First, he argued that housing market segregation affected the geographic distribution of black employment. Second, he proposed that housing market segregation increased black unemployment. Third, he proposed that metropolitan job decentralization amplified the negative effect of housing market segregation on black employment levels. The first of these three propositions followed his argument that since consumer discrimination was less likely to be an issue in the ghetto than in the suburbs, and since employers with low skill jobs were likely to locate in the ghetto because of the greater supply of low skill workers, black employment was likely to be concentrated in the ghetto.[6] The second of these three propositions stemmed from his argument that racial discrimination in the housing market imposed more job search costs on blacks than whites. These costs, such as commuting and job information costs, were more likely to limit blacks' search for work to the central city. Moreover, he argued that employers outside the ghetto, driven by white suburban consumer discrimination, may discriminate against blacks, thus further reducing blacks' chances at receiving jobs outside the ghetto.

Although Kain did not use the exact term "spatial mismatch hypothesis" to describe his third hypothesis, it is precisely this proposition that most closely refers to and that researchers have in mind when this term is used. This proposition suggests that jobs are available in metropolitan areas for which blacks would qualify, but blacks receive little information about or cannot commute to such jobs because they are located in suburbs, areas distant from blacks' residential locations. Consequently, a surplus of workers arises in the ghetto, resulting in higher ghetto unemployment if ghetto wages are inflexible.

If ghetto wages are flexible, ghetto blacks' wages should fall if they work in the ghetto and rise if they work in the suburbs. Moreover, according to Kain, workers who find jobs outside the ghetto suffer a net wage loss because of the extra commuting costs ghetto residents must pay to get to more distant jobs. Metropolitan decentralization in combination with housing market segregation, then, as Kain argued, may increase black unemployment, reduce black wage rates in the ghetto relative to the suburbs, and increase ghetto residents' commuting costs.

Kain's third hypotheses has received the most attention and has been subject to the most criticism. However, this hypothesis contains both a demand-side and a supply-side component. On the demand-side, as Jencks and Mayer (1990) note, Kain argued that the suburbanization of jobs would probably reduce employers' willingness to hire black workers because many suburban firms feared that importing black workers into white suburbs would offend white residents. On the other hand, Kain suspected that residential segregation might benefit blacks because employers in black areas might be more willing to hire blacks than employers in predominantly white or mixed areas. Thus, Kain originally tied the problem of race in labor markets to the problem of space. However, more recently, researchers have ignored the simultaneous problem of race in labor markets when examining spatial mismatches in metropolitan areas, leaving them to possibly overstate physical job access difficulties as the spatial cause of blacks' joblessness.

On the supply-side, Kain held that even if there were no employment discrimination against blacks in the suburbs, black employment probabilities would still be lower than that of whites because blacks lived farther than whites from suburban jobs and were less likely to hear about such job vacancies. However, even if blacks received suburban jobs, Kain argued, blacks would have to spend more time and money commuting to them than whites, resulting in higher unemployment rates, lower net wages, and lower labor force participation rates for blacks.

In the 1980s, the spatial mismatch hypothesis became a dominant theory of black joblessness, particularly for black men, as a result of the attention that Wilson's (1987) underclass thesis of entrenched black poverty received. The spatial mismatch hypothesis was a major structural explanation of ghetto poverty in Wilson's underclass model. In this model, the movement of central city manufacturing jobs that once provided secure employment for black men, combined with black middle-class flight to the suburbs, left behind in central cities the black poor, increasingly socially isolated from mainstream American institutions. According to Wilson, this social isolation left the black poor vulnerable to the ill effects of the spatial concentration of poverty—"dysfunctional" and aberrant behavior such as crime, out-of-wedlock births, and poor work habits.

However, it is still not altogether clear whether or to what extent the spatial mismatch of residences and jobs is a major structural problem in urban economies producing urban poverty outcomes. An understanding of the spatial mismatch hypothesis is critical because it has informed the way we think about the causes of black and Latino joblessness. This is important because joblessness, in addition to low wages, can lead to poverty. The way we think about joblessness ultimately shapes the way in which we formulate appropriate policy to deal with this problem. But if our understanding of and policy approaches to black and Latino joblessness are misdiagnosed and misstargeted, the entrapment of many blacks and Latinos in poverty in most of our major cities will likely continue, thus reinforcing the racial divide in American economic and social life.

In this chapter, I attempt to show conceptually how racial discrimination in the labor markets can confound the interpretation of studies that examine the spatial mismatch hypothesis, possibly rendering it a less weighty explanation of black and Latino joblessness. I should point out that empirical results of spatial mismatch tests have been mixed, in part due to different methodological approaches (Holzer 1991), to methodological weaknesses (Ihlanfeldt 1992), and to the choice of metropolitan area or year in these studies. I argue in this chapter that that researcher's failure to examine the extent of racial discrimination in labor markets, particularly suburban labor markets, and the motivations behind firms' location decisions may also explain why these studies have had such mixed results. Spatial mismatch studies that neglect to examine these factors will tend to confound, and, possibly, overstate, the problem of space, as measured by physical distance to jobs, in understanding black and Latino joblessness.

Most research on the spatial mismatch hypothesis has concentrated on supply-side responses to the geography of jobs (Holzer et al. 1994; Ihlanfeldt 1993; Ihlanfeldt and Sjoquist 1991). Many of these studies examine the average travel times or distances to work for different racial groups of workers and estimate how these commutes to work affect these groups' employment or wages differently. Since jobs have been moving to the suburbs from the central cities since the 1960s, and because blacks, unlike whites, remain residentially concentrated in central cities, it is assumed that blacks' employment difficulties are primarily due to their greater distance from jobs in metropolitan areas. This becomes all the more important if it is also assumed that job information declines with distance from jobs.

None of these studies, however, examine how the demand-side of the labor market (e.g., employer hiring practices and firm location decisions) affects blacks' and Latinos' ability to get a job in a spatial context. Therefore, these studies implicitly assume that the hiring playing field is even across space and that firms location decisions are not affected by racial considerations. But if discrimination in hiring against blacks and Latinos is quite extensive in suburban labor markets where jobs are located or if firms relocate out of central cities in part to distance themselves from these groups, it is difficult to determine whether central city blacks' and Latinos' inability to get suburban jobs is due to their distance to these jobs or due to suburban firms unwillingness to hire workers from these groups. That is, even if central city blacks and Latinos are fully aware of and search for suburban jobs, there is no guarantee that they will receive equal access to these jobs if suburban employers discriminate against these groups in hiring. Therefore, what might at first glance appear to be a purely spatial problem in understanding black and Latino employment difficulties may also be a problem of race.

Of course, the thrust of my argument is predicated on the existence of racial discrimination in hiring against blacks and Latinos in metropolitan labor markets, particularly as expressed in the suburbs. It is clear, then, that if the argument I am advancing is to have any weight, the problem of racial discrimination in hiring against blacks and Latinos must be established. Thus, in the remainder of this chapter, I first briefly discuss racial discrimination in labor markets to determine its existence and magnitude. Next, I examine key bodies of evidence with regard to the spatial mismatch hypothesis, paying particular attention to how race can confound the results of such studies.

IS RACE A FACTOR IN URBAN LABOR MARKETS?

When one talks about discrimination in spatial mismatch studies, most would think that housing discrimination is being discussed. Of course, housing market discrimination is assumed to exist and is explicitly theorized to be a part of the spatial mismatch explanation of black and Latino employment difficulties. There is little dispute that housing market discrimination persists, restricting blacks' and Latinos' opportunities to follow jobs (Massey and Denton 1993; Hughes and Madden 1991). However, there is evidence that employers discriminate against blacks and Latinos in the labor market (Neckerman and Kirschenman 1991; Bendick, Jr. et al. 1994). Yet, there is little discussion of how this discrimination might affect the interpretation of spatial mismatch studies.

As I have alluded to in this section, the precise form that employer hiring bias can take at the institutional level to confound interpretation of spatial mismatch studies is racial discrimination. However, it is useful to distinguish between two types of labor market discrimination: pure and statistical. In pure discrimination, either consumers, employees, or employers have a taste for discrimination that drives employers to discriminate against certain groups of workers in hiring. In other words, these groups are willing to pay a premium, in the form of prices, wages, or production costs, to distance themselves from members of certain groups. On the other hand, in statistical discrimination, employers use group membership, identified through an individual's superficial characteristics, as a representation or "proxy" for productivity traits in their hiring decisions, rather than individual productivity differences within or between groups.

In neoclassical economics, economists argue that pure discrimination is costly to employers. Neoclassicists believe that under a set of specific conditions, namely perfect competition in markets, and given a certain set of assumptions, namely, that employers have full information on the marginal productivities of workers and that workers have full information on wage and job possibilities in the labor market, employers who practice pure discrimination will likely be driven out of the market by competitors who do not practice such discrimination as long as the market is in equilibrium (Becker 1957). In statistical discrimination, however, some of these key assumptions are relaxed, such as employers' information on workers' marginal productivities. Given the relaxation of these assumptions, information on workers marginal productivities is viewed as a cost. That is, employers must spend time and money to gain more information on workers' marginal productivities during the hiring process. Under these conditions, employers, as profit maximizers, minimize the cost associated with gaining more information on workers' marginal productivities by practicing statistical discrimination. They minimize these costs by hiring workers from defined groups whose "average" marginal productivities are greater than other groups. Groups whose "average" marginal productivities are lower than other groups are statistically discriminated against by employers in hiring.

The continuing practice of discrimination in hiring as evidenced by recent research suggests that the labor market conditions needed for employers who practice pure discrimination to be driven out of the market are not being met, or it suggests that there may exist a set of conditions that certain firms face or a set of reasons that firms have that make such discrimination beneficial (Culp and Dunson 1986; Neckerman and Kirschenman 1991; Kirschenman and Neckerman 1991; Braddock and McPartland 1987; Bendick, Jr. et al. 1994). For example, Tilly and Moss (1991) argue that the practice of statistical discrimination by firms may become more severe if antidiscrimination policies make it harder to discover individual differences among applicants that employers feel are relevant. In addition, to avoid charges of reverse discrimination, particularly during times when affirmative action programs are coming under fire, firms may hire only the most qualified or overqualified blacks. Under these conditions, employers of low-wage labor might use recruitment or screening methods to distinguish between applicants that result in disadvantaging inner-city or black youth. An analysis of studies that have investigated the existence or persistence of racial discrimination in hiring suggests that statistical discrimination is the dominant form of discrimination in the labor market. Employers seem to have operationalized notions of race in distinct ways to minimize costs associated with finding out the true productivity of workers, and this practice has negatively affected blacks' and Latinos' employment opportunities (Moss and Tilly 1994; Kirschenman and Neckerman 1991; Neckerman and Kirschenman 1991).

No matter which way researchers have tested the racial discrimination thesis, most evidence shows that blacks, and to a lesser extent Latinos, are denied employment opportunities and equal wages because of the color of their skin. Recent literature has tended to use different approaches than more conventional and quantitative approaches to test for racial discrimination in the labor market and has tended to concentrate on blacks. The more conventional research on racial discrimination in labor markets investigates the possible contribution of racial discrimination in generating white-black earnings differences by examining human capital wage equations for blacks and whites. Support for or rejection of the racial discrimination thesis is determined by "decomposing" these equations to determine how much of the wage differences between these aforementioned groups is due to treatment (i.e., discrimination) or to endowments (i.e., skills, experience, and training) (Cain, 1986).

During the post-war period, white-black earnings differences shrunk, thus closing the relative racial gap in earnings. Conventional research methods tended to show that discrimination in earnings against blacks began to diminish from about 1940 to the mid-1970s, although there is considerable debate about the magnitudes. However, since the mid-1970s, white-black earnings differences began to rise, and in the 1980s blacks made little or no gains in relative earnings (Jaynes and Williams 1989). There is considerable debate about whether and to what extent racial discrimination (Boston 1988), skill differences (Bound and Freeman 1992), or quality of schooling (O'Neil 1990), among many other reasons, has contributed to this increasing racial difference in earnings.

Others have examined the role of discrimination in employment. Blacks' unemployment rate grew relative to that of whites in the 1970s and 1980s, despite the long business cycle upswing of the 1980s (Badgett 1994). Some have attributed these rising unemployment rate differences between these groups to racial differences in moving into employment from either unemployment or out of the labor force states (Juhn 1992), to a skill mismatch as a result of declining manufacturing industries in urban areas (Bound and Holzer 1991), to less effective enforcement of affirmative action policies (Leonard 1990), to blacks' increasing reliance on jobs in the secondary labor market that are characterized by high turnover (Badgett 1994), and to discrimination (Badgett 1994; Shulman 1990).

Interpretation of results from these quantitative studies provides support for or against the discrimination thesis of white-black differences in earnings or employment. However, if support is found for the discrimination thesis, one is unable to tell a story about how this discrimination takes places in an institutional context since there is nothing designed in the methods to do so. To fill this void, other researchers have used different methods to examine the existence and extent of discrimination in the labor market. These more recent studies usually examine employer hiring practices by conducting either employer interviews or audit studies.

In the first of these studies, researchers interview employers about their screening and hiring strategies, usually for low-skill jobs, and they then infer from employers' answers to questions whether or not employers engage in some sort of discrimination in hiring (Kirschenman and Neckerman 1991; Neckerman and Kirschenman 1991; and Moss and Tilly 1993). In general, these studies reveal that employers have devised hiring strategies by using social categories such as race, class and space (Neckerman and Kirschenman 1991) to distinguish potentially "productive" from "unproductive" workers. Once these distinctions are made, employers statistically discriminate against such "unproductive" workers. Employers identify black and Puerto Rican inner-city workers as the least preferred workers, while they view white, middle-class subanbanites as the most preferred. These practices seem to be more prevalent in industries with greater employee-customer contact where employers have a stronger desire for workers with "soft skills", i.e., speech, mannerisms, social skills, etc. (Moss and Tilly 1993). Although these interviews provide insights into the institutional context of discrimination, they cannot determine the extent nor the frequency of this discrimination.

The second set of studies use audit analysis to establish the existence and measure the extent of employment discrimination. These studies use matched pairs of minority, i.e., black or Latino, and white research assistants posing as applicants for the same jobs in a particular area (Bendick, Jr. et al. 1994; Fix and Struyk 1993; Turner et al. 1991). These assistants are made to look exactly alike on their resumes with respect to productivity and experience. These job candidates are also trained to act alike and to give the same responses in the pre-interview or interview stage of the job search process. Race is the only characteristic that is different between these prospective job candidates. The matched pairs of applicants, i.e., one black or Latino and one white applicant, are then sent to the same random job openings. Their treatment, whether or not they received a call back, and whether or not they got a job during the first interview or during a subsequent interview is then documented. The results are analyzed to determine whether black (Latino) and white applicants are treated differently in the pre-interview and interview stages, and to show the rate of hires for each group. After controlling to some extent for randomness in hiring, the statistical difference in the rate of hires for these racial groups is taken to be discrimination. Black and Latino applicants in Washington, DC were treated less favorably and hired less frequently than their equally qualified white counterparts more than one-fifth of the time, and a little less than one-fifth of the time, respectively (Bendick Jr. et al. 1994). Employment discrimination against blacks and Latinos was more prevalent in the farther suburbs than in the central city.

IS SPACE A BARRIER TO BLACK AND LATINO EMPLOYMENT?

It is clear from the previous discussion that racial discrimination in labor markets is a major impediment to black and Latino employment. Yet, there is little discussion on how this discrimination can affect the way in which results from spatial mismatch studies are interpreted. In the next section, I discuss spatial mismatch studies, outlining throughout the discussion the way in which racial discrimination in the labor market can confound the results of such studies. There is no straightforward way to examine this literature, so I organize the discussion by what I have defined as four major approaches to the study of spatial mismatch: central city/suburban comparisons, job decentralization, job accessibility, and firm relocation studies.

Suburban Versus Central City Residence

Some researchers use residential location, i.e., comparing the labor market outcomes of suburban and central city residents, as the main analytical approach to test the spatial mismatch hypothesis. Since employment has been moving from the central cities to suburbs over the past few decades, and because blacks remain more residentially concentrated in central cities, blacks are unable to move to suburbs to improve their employment opportunities. The expectation, then, is that those who are able to locate to suburbs should posses better employment outcomes than those who remain in the central cities.

Harrison (1972) was one of the first major critics of the spatial mismatch hypothesis. He found, as Table 2.1 shows, that in the 1960s black suburban residents' had higher unemployment rates, lower earnings, and lower occupational status than black residents in central city non-poverty tracts. But this was not true for whites as their outcomes conformed to the predictions of the standard urban model. On the other hand, Vroman and Greenfield (1980) showed that if blacks' decentralized (left central cities for suburbs) in 1973, approximately 40

Table 2.1: Median Male Earnings, Unemployment, and Occupational Status by Race and Residential Location for 12 Largest SMSAs in 1965 or 1966

Residential Location	Earnings ($/week)		Unemployment Rates (%)		Occupational Status (%)	
	White	Nonwhite	White	Nonwhite	White	Nonwhite
Central City	93.33	78.19	8.80	10.40	19.4	14.7
Poverty Areas	123.67	99.87	3.90	5.30	36.8	16.7
Suburban Ring	133.58	96.12	3.50	8.80	40.7	15.7

Source: Harrison (1974)

percent of the earnings gap between white and black males would have vanished, but none would have for females.

Based on these findings, however, conclusions must be cautiously made since neither study controlled for individual nor metropolitan area characteristics. These characteristics affect labor market outcomes and may be more important in determining outcome differences between central city and suburban residents than residential location. Price and Mills (1985) did use these controls, but found that differences in earnings between central city and suburban residents could explain no more than 6 percent of the 34 percent difference in earnings between blacks and whites.

Perhaps the early rejection of the spatial mismatch hypothesis could have resulted from the fact that a suburban residence, while being of little economic benefit in the 1960s, has become more important in getting a job over time. Jobs have continued to leave central cities since the 1970s (Kasarda 1989), possibly contributing to deeper residential and job cleavages in the 1980s than in the 1960s. Between 1967-71 black men who lived in central cities of large metropolitan areas were about as likely to work as blacks who lived in the suburbs, suggesting that black suburbanites with limited education were not much better off than their central city counterparts. But after 1969, joblessness rose steadily in both the central cities and suburbs. However, it rose much slower in the suburbs than in the central cities, so that by 1987, 49.5 percent of all black male central city residents without a high school degree were jobless compared to 33.4 percent in the suburbs (Jencks and Mayer 1990). Thus, a suburban residential location may be more important now than in the 1960s because of increasing job decentralization.

It is extremely difficult to jump to this conclusion unless one takes into account the "endogeneity" of residential location in the employment process and the selectivity of suburban migration. This "endogeneity" problem tells us that it is not altogether clear in these studies whether people who already had jobs moved to the suburbs (i.e., location endogenous), or whether people who lived in the suburbs were more likely to get jobs (i.e., location exogenous) because of greater job access. In the former case, high-skilled blacks, who tend to do well in the labor market regardless of their residential location, may have had the tendency to move to the suburbs in the 1970s and early 1980s as housing market discrimination weakened. This "selective" suburban migration could have pushed suburban residents' employment rate

The Spatial Mismatch Hypothesis Revisited

upwards, thereby causing these rates to become higher than those of central city residents. Thus, studies that do not treat residential location as an "exogenous" event in the employment process—where residents are more likely to get jobs because they live near them—will tend to bias the results towards support of the spatial mismatch hypotheses.

To deal with this "endogeneity" problem, some restrict the analysis to youth whose residential location is determined by their parents (location exogenous), although there are still questions about whether youth's unobserved characteristics are correlated with those of their parents. Using the case of youth, Ellwood (1986) found that black youth on Chicago's West side had nearly the same high unemployment rates as black youth on the South side, although there were fewer jobs in the former than in the latter area. In addition, white youths' unemployment rates were much lower than those of black youth in the West side even though both groups had equal access to jobs. As a result and although he performed no specific test, Ellwood concluded that the black youth employment problem was one of 'race, not space'. Race was also more important than residential location within U.S. central cities as well (Acs and Wissoker 1991).

On the other hand, a suburban residential location in Chicago, as opposed to different residential locations in its central city, had a strong impact on the job probability of both black and white teenagers (Ihlanfeldt and Sjoquist 1990b). Female headed households also experienced employment and wage gains as a result of having a suburban rather than a central city residential location in Chicago (Rosenbaum and Popkin 1991). However, while these results suggest that a suburban move may be a good thing for blacks in the short run, it is unclear what the long term benefits might be. If whites in the suburbs do not perceive blacks to be a threat, black suburban movers might not face employment discrimination by employers and therefore should enjoy increased employment opportunities there. However, given an increasing presence of blacks in suburbs, whites might begin to view these black residential movers as a threat. Employment discrimination against blacks in such a situation, then, might intensify (Farley 1987). In addition, white flight and job flight might also occur so that in the long run these suburban blacks might find their employment benefits decline with time.

These central city/suburban comparisons can also be rather tricky to interpret because they implicitly assume that all suburbs have uniformly enjoyed employment growth and that a suburban residential location improves the economic opportunities of all suburban households. But blacks' residential patterns within the suburban rings of most metropolitan areas are still quite limited, and, more importantly, are still quite removed from the suburban locus of employment (Kain 1992; 1985). That is, blacks are most likely to move to suburbs that are depressed and jobless (e.g., Yonkers, NY, southern Atlanta suburbs) and that closely border the central city. For blacks, then, a suburban residential location may not have any more importance in getting a job than having a central city residence. Failure to control for blacks' residential patterns in the suburbs will tend to bias results against the spatial mismatch hypothesis.

The Confounding Influence of Race Across Residential Location

I have argued in this paper that if racial discrimination in labor markets is not taken into account in spatial mismatch studies, it is very difficult to interpret the results. A simple example may help clarify this issue. Let us examine the employment rates of different groups of workers in metropolitan areas. Take two groups of workers, one group from the central city, made up of predominantly blacks, and the other from the suburbs, made up of predominantly whites, who are similar in every way, i.e., skills, age, etc., except in their residential location. In addition, let us assume that jobs are more available in the suburbs than in the central city, so that both groups of workers tend to look for employment in the suburbs. Most importantly, let us further assume that employers in the suburbs have a preference for workers from the suburbs. Given these conditions, it is expected that group members from the suburbs will be more likely to receive employment than those from the central city.

An empirical investigation into these groups' employment rates would show that the employment rate of those from the central city would be lower than that of those from the suburbs. In addition, in the metropolitan area, the white employment rate would be higher than that of blacks. One could easily infer that the employment rate of the suburban workers was higher than that of the central city workers, or that whites' employment rate was higher than that of blacks in the metropolitan area, because suburban workers lived closer to the location of job opportunities. This investigation, however, would not show how far or intensely central city workers looked for jobs in the suburbs. Because of this, statistical inference could lead to misinterpretation of the true cause of central city, mainly blacks', lower employment. In this scenario, it would be easy to confirm the spatial mismatch as the central explanation of blacks' low employment levels since it would appear that their employment problem was due to their greater distance from jobs. However, a major impediment to employment for mainly black, central city residents would be employer hiring bias against blacks. While I admit that this scenario is simplistic and omits other relevant economic factors pertinent to the analysis of labor markets, such as the likelihood of central city workers receiving suburban job information, the wage levels offered by firms, and commuting reservations wages of workers, it nevertheless does show that statistical inference into the spatial mismatch and its effect on unemployment may in fact be confounded by race (employers hiring practices).

Data on workers' search patterns would help to clarify these issues. Holzer et al. (1994) found that central city black youth travel about 1 mile less while searching for work than their white counterparts. This suggests that central city black youth may not travel greater distances to find work. This is a difficult conclusion to reach because the analysis pertains to those who found a job during the search process. Those who did not find work were not analyzed. We can assume that blacks were more likely to be jobless than whites and therefore more likely to be excluded from the analysis. Quite possibly, these jobless blacks could have searched more intensely for work than whites, became frustrated because they did not get a job, and then quit their search for work. In this situation, it is difficult to tell precisely whether or not young central city black males traveled shorter or longer distances, or traveled more often to the suburbs to find work than their white central city counterparts because we also do not know how many times search trips were made nor in what areas (i.e., suburbs) these searches took place.

Although it might be true that central city black youth travel less distance in their search for work than white youth, they may search more intensely for work. Young black males invest more time overall and use more search methods to find work than whites in either the central city or suburbs. In fact, suburban blacks spend nearly twice as long on average searching for work than comparable suburban whites (Holzer et al. 1994). This finding is consistent with the notion that racial discrimination in hiring may be more important in understanding blacks' employment difficulties than a lack of, or being farther away from, jobs.

Sorting out whether distance or discrimination is more important in preventing blacks from getting jobs can be solved in a very simple way. Comparisons of similar black and white youth labor market outcomes can be made in the same area where jobs are available for youth. If these comparisons show that white youth have better employment rates than black youth controlling for personal and family background differences, it can be inferred that race may in fact play a larger role in determining racial differences in employment than a lack of jobs (i.e., distance). This experiment is conducted in chapter 5. In short, in Prince George's County, MD, where black and Latino suburbanites live near jobs, young white men had better employment outcomes than their black or Latino counterparts controlling for personal and family background differences. This suggest that discrimination is more important than distance from jobs in preventing blacks and Latinos from receiving jobs. However, Prince George's County residents had better employment rates than their Washington, DC, or central-city, counterparts, suggesting that space is important in getting a job as well. But there were greater differences between Prince George's and DC's residents employment rate for young white than black or Latino men. Also, racial differences in employment between whites and blacks (Latinos) were much greater in Prince George's County than in Washington, DC. This suggest that more severe employer discrimination against young black and Latino men in Prince George's County (e.g., the suburbs) than in Washington, DC, rather than a lack of jobs, was an equally likely explanation of racial differences in employment. Audit studies discussed earlier also showed that racial discrimination against blacks and Latinos was much greater in Washington, DC's suburbs than in the DC itself (Bendick, Jr. et. al. 1994).

Employer based interviews also support the notion that greater racial discrimination in suburban labor markets is a cause of greater racial employment differences in metropolitan areas. This research suggests that employers try to avoid workers who are black, and to a lesser extent Latino, and come from the central city (Kirschenman and Neckerman 1991). But suburban employers who cannot determine whether or not a low-skill black or Latino worker is from the suburbs will tend to statistically discriminate against all black and Latino workers regardless of their true residential location to eliminate the possibility that they might come from the central city. Given these hiring practices, spatial mismatch studies that fail to examine such practices are difficult to interpret. Under these circumstances, it is difficult to determine whether or not the absence of black and Latino workers in suburban firms is due to spatial frictions such as the inability of these groups to get suburban job information or commute to suburban jobs if they live in the central city, or to discrimination in hiring against blacks and Latinos by suburban employers.

Job Decentralization

There are other ways to examine the spatial mismatch hypothesis. One could estimate the effect of job decentralization, meaning the degree to which jobs are suburbanized in metropolitan areas, on white, black, and Latino labor market outcome measures. If the extent of job decentralization has more negative effects on black and Latino than white labor market outcomes in the central city, evidence is found in support of the spatial mismatch hypothesis.

Initial job decentralization studies found little support for the spatial mismatch hypothesis. Mooney (1969) in response to Kain's (1968) spatial mismatch proposition found that black employment rose with the fraction of blacks working in the suburbs and with the low levels of job decentralization. However, the negative effect of the metropolitan unemployment rate on blacks' employment was much greater than that of the job decentralization effect. Offner and Saks (1971), Freidlander (1972) and Masters (1974) also found limited support for the job decentralization hypothesis. More recent analysis, however, has shown support for the job decentralization hypothesis. Farley (1987) found that black and Latino unemployment rates were lower relative to those of whites in metropolitan areas where jobs were least suburbanized and where blacks and Latinos were least concentrated in central cities. It is likely then that the spatial mismatch has become more pronounced over time.

Like central city/suburban comparison methods, conclusions from these job decentralization studies are difficult to make since they do not use individual data to control for differences between people that can also contribute to racial differences in labor market outcomes. Ihlanfeldt and Sjoquist (1989) controlled for individual differences and found that the decentralization of low-skilled jobs decreased the earnings of less-educated black and white males and to a lesser extent females. However, because they examined those with earnings, they, by extension, excluded those who were not employed. Those who are jobless might be more affected by the scarcity of relevant central city jobs, and their exclusion from job decentralization studies might have biased the results of such studies.

This discussion raises questions about which labor market outcome measure should be used in job decentralization studies. For example, most researchers use either employment or unemployment measures. However, we might be better able to asses the effect of job decentralization in generating racial differences in employment outcomes if we decomposed the unemployment rate into its component parts. In this way, we could determine where the significant racial differences in unemployment are being generated. Incidence, frequency, and duration of unemployment—the components of unemployment—are mathematically related to the unemployment rate (Suits and Morgenstern 1967). Moreover, unemployment duration is the most crucial component of observed unemployment rates of youth and adults alike (Clark and Summers, 1979). The duration of unemployment, then, might be a more accurate indicator of blacks' employment problems in relation to those of whites.

Holzer et al. (1994) used the duration of unemployment as the labor market outcome measure and found that job decentralization had substantially more negative effects on black than white youth unemployment. But they analyzed only those who eventually found work within a one year period, excluding those youth who remained unemployed by the end of the year. Black youth tend to have longer unemployment durations than comparable white youth (Clark and Summers 1979). Black youth with long uncompleted unemployment duration spells, then, were excluded from this analysis. Thus, the results for blacks are likely biased towards the job decentralization thesis since only the most employable blacks, or those most likely to respond to the presence of jobs in the central city, were included their study. In chapter 4, I include those who were both unemployed and out of the labor force in an analysis, but still find that job decentralization was associated with young black males' longer jobless durations. However, as we shall examine later, race, or the treatment of young black and Latino males in the labor market, was equally or more important in generating blacks' and Latinos' longer jobless durations.

Why do Firms Move in the First Place?

Race may not only be more important than job decentralization in understanding blacks' and Latinos' inability to get jobs, it may also influence firms' location decisions. If it does, interpreting results from job decentralization studies becomes rather difficult. Firms may decide to relocate from the central city to the suburbs not only because of cheaper land prices and lower taxes, and a better quality work force (Whyte 1988), but also because of problems in the central city that they may in fact link to race, such as crime or high black unemployment. Racial factors are important in firms location decisions (Cole and Deskins 1988). Thus, the causal arrows in job decentralization studies may be blurred. That is, it is not clear whether job decentralization is the cause of black and Latino unemployment or whether black and Latino unemployment is in part caused by employers' decisions to leave central cities for suburbs because they want to distance themselves from black and Latino populations.

This suggests that space may be used as a tool by firms to limit contact with blacks and Latinos. But irrespective of how distance is created between jobs and black residential locations, it still may be an employment barrier that makes it difficult for blacks to both gain information about jobs and commute to work. While this is true, it is the policy implications of the problem's source that is at issue. If employers use space as a tool to minimize contact with black or Latino populations, distance mitigating policies, such as population dispersal programs or transportation policies that are designed to make jobs accessible to blacks and Latinos, are likely to fail. Under these conditions, employers are likely to devise new strategies to distance themselves from these populations if such policies are adopted.

Job Accessibility

An analysis of direct job accessibility offers yet another strategy to test the spatial mismatch hypothesis. These kinds of studies generally consider zones or census tracts within a metropolitan area and use average travel time (commuting time), distance, or job availability as a measure of job access. If black or Latino job access measures are more positively correlated with their unemployment than in the case of whites, then part of the unemployment rate difference between blacks (Latinos) and whites can be attributed to their poorer job access.

Early studies showed small, negative effects of job access on employment (and labor force participation) for whites and blacks in Pittsburgh (Hutchinson 1974, 1978). Consistent with the mismatch story, the negative effects for blacks were much stronger than those for whites. On the other hand, more recent studies showed that there was little job accessibility differences between blacks and whites in Washington, DC (Green and James 1993). A major weakness in these studies is that they do not take into account the "endogeneity" of residential location in the employment process that I discussed earlier. These studies are difficult to interpret because it is not clear whether people with jobs moved closer to their jobs or whether people without jobs moved where jobs are located and then received jobs. In the former case, the distance or travel time to work that is being measured is generated by workers' choice to live near or far from their job rather than being generated by whether they live near or far from jobs. High-skill workers are likely to live farther from work than low-skill workers since they have better job information and can afford more distant trips. Because workers of all skill levels were included in these analysis, it is difficult to accept the conclusions of these studies. Without controlling for residential "endogeneity" and workers' skill levels, the results of job access studies are likely biased in favor of the spatial mismatch hypothesis.

Taylor and Ong (1995) analyzed low-skill workers and found that black and Latino workers had shorter commuting times and distances to work than whites in U.S. metropolitan areas. They concluded that no support was found for the spatial mismatch hypothesis. Counter to their interpretation, their findings do not necessarily contradict this hypothesis. Under spatial mismatch, blacks' travel distances to work can be shorter or longer than those of whites. Their results are inconsistent with the existence of spatial mismatch only if we assume that blacks and Latinos were fully informed of all job openings in metropolitan areas. But if we make a reasonable assumption that job information declines with distance from jobs, so that those who live farther away from job centers are less likely to hear or know about job openings than those who live near them. Let us further assume that blacks and Latinos live farther away from jobs than whites. Given these assumptions, blacks and Latinos who searched for but did not get or maintain a job in suburban areas because of distance related problems may have dropped out of the labor force leaving behind those who only searched for and received work in minority areas. In this case, a spatial mismatch of jobs and residences is indeed responsible for blacks' and Latinos' shorter commuting times and distances to work than whites.

Restricting the analysis to youth might be the best way to address these problems because they are generally low-skilled and have their residential locations "exogenously" determined by their parents. Also, because they perform more poorly in the labor market and have more difficulty commuting to work than their adult counterparts, the spatial mismatch may be more a problem for youth than adults. Ellwood (1986) used three direct measures of job access to test the spatial mismatch hypothesis for youth in Chicago. He found very small, but positive effects of job access on the employment rate for two access variables, and no effect for the third. Results from his analysis have been frequently cited as conclusive evidence against the spatial mismatch hypothesis because of the extensive job access variables used in the study.

Others have found support for the spatial mismatch hypothesis using the case of youth. Results of these studies indicate that the fraction off the racial gap in employment attributable to job access ranged from one-third to one-half depending on the group used (Ihlanfeldt 1992, 1993; Ihlanfeldt and Sjoquist 1990a, 1991). For example, Table 2.2 shows that black and Latino youth have longer commute times to work than whites and that their employment rates were lower than that of whites. Thus, if blacks (Latinos) travel time to work was made the same as that of whites, their employment rate would rise and the racial gap between blacks (Latinos) and whites employment rate would fall (see last column). The divergent results between these studies are likely due to the metropolitan area chosen for the analysis and to the fact that Ellwood, unlike Ihlanfeldt and Sjoquist, did not control for individual or family background differences.

Travel time to work is not only a function of how far jobs are located from worker's residences, but also a function of what transportation mode is used. Travel time differences between black (Latino) and white youth might be determined by whether these youth have less access to private transportation than comparable white youth. Blacks spend more time traveling to work than whites, but cover less distance, particularly in the case of males. This is because blacks are less likely than whites to travel to work in cars, a faster mode of transportation (Holzer et al. 1994). Having access to or owning a car might improve one's ability to get a job because cars offer more mobility and flexibility than other modes of transportation. But it is

Table 2.2: Mean Travel Times, Employment Rates, and the Share of Racial Employment Gap Explained by Predicted Travel Time Differences in 1980: Logit Models

Category	Mean Travel Time	Employment Rate	Percentage Change in Employment Rate Gap from Substitution of WT for B(L)T Logit
16–19 Years Old Not Enrolled			
White	18.58	.418	—
Black	24.40	.190	-27
Latino	22.60	.292	-35
20–24 Years Old At Home			
White	18.80	.786	—
Black	24.40	.508	-22
Latino	22.86	.658	-26

Source: Ihlanfeldt (1992)
Note: WT = white time; BT = black time; LT = Latino time

The Spatial Mismatch Hypothesis Revisited

difficult to conclude that blacks are less likely to get jobs because they have less access to cars than whites. Access to cars or car ownership reflects the ability get jobs. To own a car one must pay. But if one cannot get a job, one cannot pay for a car since it is by working that one gets income. Thus, car ownership depends on having a job and having a job depends on owning a car. Thus, controlling for car ownership in these studies may in fact be controlling for other factors that determine having access to jobs such as discrimination.

The larger question of these studies is that they do not investigate the possible role that race may play in causing blacks' and Latinos' distance or travel time to work to be longer than that of whites. First, part of the black and Latino mean travel time may in fact measure employer discrimination in the labor market. If blacks and Latinos travel father to work than whites because employer discrimination limits their job opportunities, part of black travel time may in fact reflect employer discrimination. Leonard (1987) found this to be true in his study of job access in Los Angeles. Second, blacks' and Latinos' poorer job access than that of whites could be attributable in part to employers desire to distance themselves from black and Latino populations. In this case, blacks' and Latinos' longer travel times and distances to work than whites cannot simply be attributed to a benign sense of physical distance from jobs, but to employer location decisions that create distance between jobs and black and Latino residential locations.

Firm Relocation

Finally, others use the event of a relocating firm to examine the spatial mismatch hypothesis. Usually, these studies examine the impact of a firm's move from the central city to the suburbs on employees' employment, commuting time or distances traveled to work. Inferences can be drawn from these results that either confirm or reject the spatial mismatch hypothesis.

Zax and Kain (1991) examined eight years of employment records from 1971 to 1978, including the records for new hires, of a particular service industry firm located in Detroit's Central Business District. During the fourth year, the firm moved to Dearborn, which is a suburb of Detroit and directly adjacent to Detroit's city border. They examined the effects of the firm's relocation on workers' moves, quits, and commuting adjustments. They termed 'winners' those whose commute times from their original residences were reduced by the firm relocation, while they termed 'losers' those whose commute times were increased. They found that white 'losers' responded to the relocation by quitting their jobs. On the other hand, black 'losers' were far more likely to quit than black winners. However, blacks were more likely to quit than comparable whites because of the longer commuting times that they had to travel to get to the new job location. This evidence was taken as support for the spatial mismatch hypothesis.

While this study is unique in comparison to other spatial mismatch studies, the researchers make a great leap in their conclusions. After the firm's relocation, the observed higher quit rate of blacks relative to whites may not necessarily imply that blacks' residential choices were constrained in the suburbs or that there was a greater negative effect on blacks imposed by the firm's move. To determine this, one needs to know what happened to those who quit. If blacks who quit went on to equal or better jobs than whites who quit, then Zax and Kain overstate the effect of the spatial mismatch. If, however, whites who quit did better but no worse than blacks who quit, then their interpretation understates the effect of the spatial mismatch. In order to resolve these issues, additional data must be obtained from those who quit. In addition, it is not clear why the firm moved. If it moved to distance itself from a labor force that it deemed problematic, such conclusions reached by Zax and Kain are thus simply reflective of the firm's preference to be near or far from certain groups.

Like other spatial mismatch studies we have discussed, the larger issue that is left unresolved by these kinds of studies is that firms' motivations to relocate are not taken into account. Again, it is likely that firms move to the suburbs because they want to distance themselves from predominantly black and Latino populations. In this case, distance may be a tool that employers use to rid themselves of black and Latino workers.

Fernandez (1994) analyzed a firm that moved to the suburbs for reasons other than to distance itself from minority populations or to rid itself of its minority workers. In his longitudinal study of a Milwaukee food-processing plant—which, at the time, was moving from the city's Central Business District to the suburban ring—he found that plant relocation had the potential to induce mismatches between workers' residences and jobs, and that these mismatches would be most severe for minorities. However, the extremely small sample sizes of minority workers in Fernandez' study makes it difficult to accept the generalizeability of such studies on the average minority worker's response to a firm relocation. In addition, it is difficult to control for the fact that this firm may have had unique characteristics which made it difficult for minority workers to follow the firm's move. The reconciliation of these issues can only be achieved by the convergence of results from many more similar studies.

Spatial Mismatch in the Youth Labor Market

Researchers also use the case of youth to investigate the spatial mismatch's role in determining higher black unemployment. They do so for a number of reasons, some of which I have mentioned throughout this chapter. First, researchers use the case of youth to overcome the simultaneity problem between residential location and employment. They restrict the sample to youth because in most instances their residential locations can be considered an exogenous event, that is, it is decided by their parent(s). Furthermore, it is unlikely that the employment status of a young person influences a parents decision of where or when to move.[7] Second, it is also the case that youth perform more poorly in the labor market, have more difficulty commuting since fewer of them have means to private transportation, and receive less job information than their adult counterparts. Given this, one should expect that the spatial mismatch may be more of a problem for youth than their adult counterparts. Third, racial unemployment differentials are much larger for youth in relation to their adult counterparts. Finally, as Ihlanfeldt (1990) notes, because of black youth's extremely high unemployment rates, there is much more policy concern for the possible consequences of this high unemployment on future employment, i.e., scarring effects. That is, because youth are unable to maintain stable work patterns, or get job skills and work attitudes as a result of high unemployment, they are more likely to experience higher unemployment and lower wages as they age in the labor market.

Osterman (1980) investigated the relative importance of the spatial mismatch and hiring-queue hypotheses in determining high levels of black youth joblessness. The hiring-queue hypothesis holds that employers rank groups of workers according to their preferences and hire on the basis of this rank ordering. Hiring is based on group membership rather than on individual productivity differences of members within groups. Effectively, then, employers rank workers according to their group membership by preference. Ranking of groups is, in part, determined by the groups' average productivity profile. This ranking causes a hiring queue to take form. Osterman was interested in whether women and white youth were in competition with black youth for jobs. Using separate equations for black and white youth, he regressed the employment and labor force participation rate on the ratio of jobs in the central city to those in the suburbs, divided by the ratio of the population of the central city to the population of the suburbs and on variables to measure competition from adult women and youth. He found that a small part of the labor market outcome differential between blacks and whites is attributable to employer preferences for adult women and white youth. However, he found that job decentralization was not important in explaining the racial differentials for labor market outcomes, thus offering no support for the spatial mismatch hypothesis.

Osterman's model was criticized on two accounts (Ihlanfeldt 1990). First, he did not include variables that measured individual and family background differences among the youth. This is a valid criticism since individual and family background differences are also important determinants of racial youth employment differentials. Second, his measure of job decentralization was viewed as being too crude since it included all jobs rather than only jobs for which youth are qualified to hold. Ellwood (1982), using direct measures of job access, also tested the spatial mismatch hypothesis. He found no significant impacts of job access on youth's employment, which led him to reject "space" and accept "race" as the primary determinant of black youths' employment problems.

Leonard (1986) was the first to criticize Ellwood's work. He suggested that since the job access measures were based on small samples, the small magnitude of the job access coefficients may have reflected measurement error. Also, like Osterman's study, Ellwood used data aggregated over zones within the Chicago area. Thus, he could not adequately account for individual and family background differences between black and white youths that may have also caused racial differences in labor market outcomes.

In response to the methodological weaknesses of previous spatial mismatch studies, Ihlanfeldt (1992, 1993) and Ihlanfeldt and Sjoquist (1990, 1991a) have published a series of articles examining the impact of job accessibility on youth employment. All of their research supports the view that the spatial mismatch is a cause of black youth's low employment levels, contradicting the findings of both Osterman and

Ellwood. Their analyses of youth unemployment used individual data to control for individual and family differences and divides metropolitan areas into residential zones to construct their main independent variable for job access. This variable is measured by the mean travel time of low-wage workers who traveled to work by private, motorized carrier and lived in the same residential zone as the individual youth. In all of their studies, their results indicate that the fraction off the racial gap in employment attributable to job access ranged from one-third to one-half depending on the group used.

Travel time to work is not only a function of how far jobs are located from worker's residences, but also a function of what transportation mode a worker uses. Thus, travel time differences between black and white youth could result from not only whether blacks live farther from jobs than whites, but also whether black youth have less access to private transportation than white youth. Holzer et al. (1994) attempt to sort this puzzle out by examining the work, search and travel behavior of white and black youth. They examine the effect of transportation mode on miles and time spent traveling to work for white and black youth. They found that blacks spent more time traveling to work than whites, but covered less distance, particularly for males. Moreover, differences in distances traveled while searching for work were no different than those while working. Therefore, the time cost per mile traveled was significantly higher for blacks. They also concluded that part of this higher cost could be accounted for by the lower rates of automobile ownership among blacks. Because their sample included both youth who lived home and who were on their own, and because they conducted no test to verify whether or not this fact made any difference in the results, these results may be biased. For example, if white youth in the sample were more likely to live on their own than black youth, and if white youth who were on their own were more likely to have a job than comparable black youth, and if, finally, white youth were more likely to move near that job, then the miles traveled and time spent travelling to work differences between white and black youth would have been less likely to be caused by a lack of nearby jobs and would rather have been caused by whites' greater likelihood of getting jobs and their greater ability to move near them.

These studies also suffer from methodological weaknesses although they do improve on previous job access studies. First, although these studies do control for the endogeneity problem of residential and job location by limiting their sample to youth who live at home, and although they all control for individual and family background differences that can also explain racial differences in employment, most do not adequately control for metropolitan area differences that can also influence racial differences in employment.

Secondly, travel time, although at first glance it may appear to resolve some of the methodological and measurement issues surrounding investigation of the spatial mismatch, does suffer from three main weaknesses. First, there may be no relation between travel time to work and the extent to which jobs are available nearby. However, this may be more true for high income adults who may live in the suburbs and work in the central city, for example, than for youth. Secondly, the mean travel time measure can only be estimated from those who have a job. Since blacks are more likely to be jobless than whites, it is likely that these measures are more biased in the black samples, and thus may lead to measurement error. Thirdly, and most importantly, part of the black mean travel time may in fact be measuring employer discrimination in the labor market. If blacks have to travel father to work than whites because employer discrimination limits their job opportunities, part of black travel time may in fact reflect employer discrimination. This point will be expanded in the next section.

CONCLUSION

What have we learned about the Kain's three hypotheses some thirty years later? First, there is little controversy over Kain's first hypothesis, that is, there is little dispute over whether residential segregation affects the geographical distribution of black employment. Second, there is some controversy over Kain's second hypothesis, that residential segregation harms black economic welfare in the labor market. Third, there is controversy over Kain's third hypothesis that a spatial mismatch between blacks' residential locations and job locations hurts blacks' labor market outcomes and explains much of the differences between white and black labor market outcomes in metropolitan areas. The results of spatial mismatch studies are mixed, in part due to the different methods used by researchers, in part due to the index used to measure the spatial mismatch, in part due to the metropolitan area examined, and in part due to the time period selected to examine this issue. However, there is agreement that employed blacks have higher commuting times to work than do comparable employed whites.

Nonetheless, there is still uncertainty as to whether these commuting differences really reflect job accessibility problems as a result of distances from work and whether they are large enough to explain racial unemployment differentials. What is also unclear is the relative importance of the spatial mismatch effect when compared to race discrimination in explaining racial unemployment differentials.

Statistical discrimination against black youth in hiring, based primarily on race but also on space and class, affects the way in which we should think about the evidence assembled from spatial mismatch studies. Evidence of discriminatory practices suggests that the playing field of potential youth workers may not be even in the suburbs or central cities. What researchers may in fact be showing is not only the effect of space or physical distance to job opportunities on black or Latino youth's likelihood of getting a job, but also the effect of employer discrimination. So what originally may appear to be simply a mismatch problem between blacks' residential location and the location of employment may actually be more a problem of race discrimination in the labor market. In this instance, the problem of race confounds the problem of space, and if the problem of race is not acknowledged, the problem of space, though important, will be overstated.

CHAPTER 3
Does Living in the Suburbs Really Make a Difference?
Residential Location and the Dynamic Labor Market Outcomes of Young Males

As we learned in the previous chapter, the spatial mismatch has become a dominant explanation of blacks', and to some extent Latinos', low employment levels both absolutely and relative to that of whites in metropolitan areas. In this chapter, the spatial mismatch hypothesis is examined by comparing the dynamic labor market outcomes of young males' in the suburbs and central cities. A key prediction is implicit in the spatial mismatch idea. The hypothesis suggests that suburban residents should perform better in the labor market than their central city counterparts, and that this should be particularly true for blacks, and to some extent Latinos, because of the role that housing market discrimination plays in limiting their housing options.

Few studies have compared the labor market outcomes of black central city and suburban residents. Those that have are over twenty years old. Harrison (1972) compared the frequency distribution of unemployment rates among male workers who resided in central city poverty areas, the rest of the central city, and the suburban ring. He found that place of residence had no effect on the unemployment of blacks, and argued, instead, that racial discrimination in the labor market against blacks accounted for blacks' high unemployment rate. More recently, Bluestone et al. (1992) compared the labor market outcomes for 20 year-old out-of-school men with limited schooling in the central city and suburbs and found that white and black suburban male jobless rates were lower in the suburbs than in the central cities. These results suggest, as Jencks and Mayer (1990) note, that perhaps the spatial mismatch has become more pronounced since the 1960s. Nonetheless, suburban residence has not been shown to improve blacks' labor market outcomes relative to their white counterparts. Bluestone et. al. (1994) found that black males' jobless rates are significantly greater than their white male counterparts in both the central cities and suburbs, and that no ground in these measures was made up by blacks if they lived in the suburbs as opposed to the central city.

These studies use static or aggregate measures of unemployment. These measures, while they paint a broad picture of the labor market difficulties of blacks and central city residents, cannot, by their very nature, convey the complexity of their unemployment dynamics. These measures do not allow one to determine, for example, whether unemployment reflects long spells of unemployment of a few people or whether it reflects short unemployment spells by many people. Clark and Summers (1979) showed how unemployment dynamics are important to understanding aggregate unemployment. However, since it was not their intention, they did not investigate these differences between central city and suburban residents and between blacks and whites in these areas. In addition, no studies of unemployment dynamics and residential location of which I am aware have included Latinos. In fact, as Tienda (1994) notes, a big research gap with respect to understanding Latinos in the labor market is the lack of knowledge about Latinos' unemployment dynamics. Knowledge of these unemployment dynamics, in general, and, by place of residence, in particular, should also help our understanding of growing Latino unemployment and joblessness as well.

The data used in the analysis is from the National Longitudinal Survey of Labor Market Experience of Youth (NLSY).[8] In order to calculate unemployment dynamics, i.e., spells and duration of unemployment, I measured the completed spells of unemployment and jobless categories by arraying the weekly labor market information from the beginning of the 1984 interview to the beginning of the 1985 interview, and then selected only those spells of unemployment and joblessness that began and ended during this period. In addition, the number of spells each individual may have had during the interview year can also be measured. I restricted the analysis to male civilian, out-of-school, young adults with less than two years of college and living in either the central city or suburb of a Standard Metropolitan Statistical Area (SMSA). Recent literature suggests that out-of-school, young male adults with limited schooling, skills, and labor market experience are more likely to experience labor market difficulties (Bound and Freeman 1992; Holzer 1993) and are more likely to be affected by a spatial mismatch of jobs and residential location (Bluestone et al. 1994; Ihlanfeldt, 1992). I use data from the 1985 interview year because it was most recent post-recession year with dynamic employment data for youth. The ages of the young adult males in this sample are 19 to 27.[9]

JOBLESSNESS IN CENTRAL CITIES AND SUBURBS

A key assumption in this exercise is that job opportunities are greater for youth in the suburbs than the central city. In the next chapter we provide evidence that jobs, particularly those jobs in industries in which youth work, continue to move from central cities to suburbs. If this is true, we should expect those youth who live in the suburbs to do much better than their central city counter parts in the labor market because of their greater physical proximity to jobs. Many investigations that compare the labor market employment outcomes of racial groups invariably examine unemployment rates. Table 3.1 shows the unemployment and jobless rates for the sample of out-of-school, young adult males with limited schooling by race and residential location.[10] In the urban areas as a whole, young white males' unemployment rate, 10.0 percent, is substantially lower than that of young blacks and Latinos, 25.2 and 15.0 percent, respectively. The same is also true for the jobless rate.

If we examine these rates by residential location we find some interesting results. Young suburban males' unemployment rates are lower in the suburbs than in the central cities. It is precisely these findings that make the spatial mismatch hypothesis an attractive explanation of blacks' and Latinos' high unemployment in metropolitan areas. Blacks and Latinos are more likely to live in the central cities, where unemployment rates are high in relation to those in the suburbs, while whites are more likely to live in the suburbs, where unemployment rates are low in relation to those in the central cities. These initial results provide some support for the hypothesis as an explanation of blacks' and Latinos' high unemployment in relation to that of whites in metropolitan areas.

Young, suburban white males' unemployment rate, however, is 33 percent lower than that of their central city counterparts, while suburban black and Latino males' unemployment rate is only 7 and 10.3 percent, respectively, lower than that of their central city counterparts. Thus, suburban white males are substantially better off compared to their central city counterparts with respect to the unemployment rate than either young blacks or Latinos. Given this, it is not surprising that the black/white and Latino/white unemployment ratio is greater in the suburbs, 3.10 and 1.84, respectively, than in the central city, 2.50 to 1.52, respectively. These results are interesting since it was anticipated that these ratios would be larger in the suburbs. Thus, these initial results cast some doubt on the spatial mismatch hypothesis to explain racial differences in labor market outcomes in metropolitan areas. Firm conclusions, however, cannot be made until one controls for differences in personal characteristics that could also contribute to suburban/central city differences.

Table 3.1: Unemployment and Jobless Rates by Race and Residential Location: 1984

		Unemployment	Jobless
White		10.0	15.0
	central city	10.5	15.4
	suburb	7.9	12.9
Black		25.2	32.9
	central city	26.2	33.1
	suburb	24.5	35.1
Latino		15.0	24.4
	central city	16.0	26.1
	suburb	14.5	20.9
Total		12.8	18.7
	central city	14.7	20.7
	suburb	9.4	14.9

In both the central city and suburbs, white males' jobless rate is substantially lower than that of either blacks or Latinos. However, suburban blacks' jobless rate is 6 percent higher than that of their central city counterparts, while the jobless rate is 19 and 25 percent lower for suburban whites and Latinos, respectively, compared to that

Does Living in the Suburbs Really Make a Difference?

of their central city counterparts. Thus, while the Latino/white jobless ratio remains stable at 1.70 in both the central city and suburb, the black/white jobless ratio rises, as it does for the unemployment ratio, from 2.15 in the central city to 2.72 in the suburbs. Thus, given this evidence, it is difficult to initially support the spatial mismatch hypothesis as an explanation for black's higher joblessness.

Given this brief examination of the unemployment and jobless rates by residential location, it is not entirely clear that blacks' and Latinos' employment prospects are better in the suburbs than in the central cities. Blacks' unemployment rate is slightly lower in the suburbs than in the central city. However, their jobless rate is 6 percent higher in the suburbs than in the central city, suggesting that young blacks are more likely to become discouraged and leave the labor force in the suburbs than in the central cities most likely because of an inability to find work. Why they may do so is not clear from this table. In the case of Latinos, residence in the suburbs seems to improve their unemployment and jobless rates by 10 and 24 percent, respectively, suggesting that their employment prospects are better in the suburbs. However, both black and Latino males' unemployment and jobless rates are substantially worse than those of their white counterparts in either the central city or suburbs. In fact, young black males' rates are worse than those of their white counterparts in the suburbs than in the central city. A closer examination of unemployment dynamics may help us to identify the sources that differentiate young white, black and Latino males' unemployment and jobless rates across space.

DIMENSIONS OF JOBLESSNESS IN CENTRAL CITIES AND SUBURB

The unemployment rate is a static measure that does not provide much information about the dynamics of unemployment. Although the unemployment rate is generally expressed as a single percentage, it is actually made up of three distinct factors. The unemployment rate is not only determined by the number of people who are unemployed at any particular time, it is also made up of the number of people who become unemployed at one time or another during the course of the year and by how long they stay unemployed. The percentage of individuals who become unemployed sometime during the year is termed the "incidence of unemployment." The "frequency", or the number of spells of unemployment per individual during the year, is another dimension of unemployment. The final component of unemployment is its "duration," or the time that a given spell of unemployment lasts. Table 3.2 shows these dimensions of unemployment by race and residential location.

The incidence, frequency, and duration of unemployment are mathematically linked to and determine the unemployment rate. Suits and Morgenstern (1967) showed that incidence (N), frequency (S), and duration (D) of unemployment are mathematically related to the unemployment rate (U) by the equation:

$$U = (N \times S \times D)/52. \qquad (3.1)$$

For example, as Table 3.2 shows, when 50.8 percent young black males in the central city labor force experienced one bout of unemployment and when their average number of spells of unemployment was 1.32, and when their average duration of unemployment was 20.3 weeks, their unemployment rate was:

$$U = (50.8 \times 1.32 \times 20.3)/52 = 26.2,$$

which we also saw in Table 3.1.

A number of interesting results are found in Table 3.2. First, young white males in both the central city and suburbs have more spells of unemployment than blacks in the central city or suburbs and Latinos in the central city. However, their unemployment durations are shorter than either young black or Latino males in both residential areas. These counterintuitive result suggests that young white males have less difficulty getting jobs in the central city and suburbs than either black males in these areas or Latino males in the central city. Young white males in either the suburbs or central city appear to be able to experiment more in the labor market by searching for better jobs with a significantly lower "cost" of unemployment than either young black or Latino males. If they quit jobs in search of better ones, their risk of being unemployed for a long period of time is relatively small. At the same time, if they are laid off or fired from a job, their risk of being unemployed for a long period of time may also be very small. However, the same pattern is not true for either black or Latino males. If they quit, or are fired or laid off from a job, their return to work rate appears much lower than that for whites, suggesting that their risk of longer unemployment, or their "cost" of being unemployed, is much greater than that of whites, particularly in the central city.

Table 3.2: Dimensions of Unemployment by Race and Residential Location: 1984

	Central City	Suburb	Total
	Whites		
Duration (weeks)	14.6	13.7	14.5
Frequency (spell)	1.43	1.44	1.42
Incidence (%)	26.1	20.9	25.2
Turnover rate (%)	37.3	30.1	35.8
	Blacks		
Duration (weeks)	20.3	19.2	19.6
Frequency (spell)	1.32	1.34	1.33
Incidence (%)	50.8	49.4	50.2
Turnover rate (%)	67.1	67.7	66.8
	Latinos		
Duration (weeks)	16.0	16.5	16.5
Frequency (spell)	1.33	1.43	1.36
Incidence (%)	39.1	31.9	34.8
Turnover rate (%)	52.0	45.6	47.3
	Total		
Duration (weeks)	16.4	14.4	15.7
Frequency (spell)	1.38	1.43	1.39
Incidence (%)	33.8	23.7	30.5
Turnover rate (%)	46.6	33.9	42.4

Young white males duration of unemployment is nearly 6 and 2 weeks shorter than that of young black and Latino males, respectively, in either the central city or suburbs. As a result, the black/white and Latino/white unemployment duration ratio remains fairly constant at about 1.40 and 1.10, respectively, in both the central city and suburbs.

Given that young black and Latino males possess longer unemployment durations, fewer spells of unemployment, and higher unemployment rates than their white counterparts in both the central city and suburbs, it is easy to deduce that their incidence of unemployment is greater than comparable whites in both areas. Table 3.2 shows that this is indeed is case. The percentage of young black and Latino males who ever become unemployed during some part of the year is two and one-and-a-half times greater, respectively, than comparable whites in both residential areas.

Another indicator of the dynamics of unemployment is the "turnover rate." Barrett and Morgenstern (1974) defined the "turnover rate," or the flow rate of individuals into unemployment, as the product of incidence and frequency, or:

turnover rate = incidence x spells. (3.2)

It is interpreted as the probability that a person will experience unemployment in a given period. For example, as Table 3.2 shows, 39.1 percent of young Latino males in the central city had at least one bout of unemployment in 1984, while they had on average 1.33 spells of unemployment. Thus, young Latino males' turnover rate in the central city was:

turnover rate = 39.1 x 1.33 = 52.0.

Table 3.2 also shows this measure for males in both central city and suburbs. It is not surprising, given our results of unemployment duration, incidence, and frequency, that black and Latino males' probability of experiencing unemployment during the year is greater than that of comparable whites in both the central city and suburbs. Young Latino males' turnover rate is lower in the suburbs than in the central city, suggesting that their probability of having a bout of unemployment is lower in the suburbs. This is also true for white males. However, black males' turnover rate is about the same in the suburbs and central city, suggesting their probability of having a bout of unemployment is the same in both areas. However, both the black/white and Latino/white turnover rate ratio is greater in the suburbs, 2.25 and 1.51, respectively, than in the central city, 1.80 and 1.39, respectively.

Clark and Summers (1979) showed that there is little difference in the states of unemployed and not-in-the-labor-force for those who are able to work. Table 3.3 is included to compare the labor market experiences of those unemployed and jobless. This table compares the mean weeks of unemployment and jobless durations of young males in the central city and suburbs. Like unemployment duration, young white males' jobless durations are shorter than those of either black or Latino males in both the central city and suburbs. Moreover, the black/white jobless duration ratio, like the black/white unemployment duration ratio, remains constant at about 1.41 in both the central city and suburbs, suggesting that blacks' residence in the suburbs does little to reduce racial differences in unemployment or joblessness. The Latino/white jobless duration ratio, however, decreases from 1.29, in the central city to 1.11 in the suburbs, suggesting that living in the suburbs may improve young Latinos' employment prospects in relation to those of their white, suburban counterparts.

Table 3.3: Mean Weeks Unemployment and Jobless Duration by Race and Residential Location: 1984

		Unemployment	Jobless
White		14.5	22.2
	central city	14.6	22.4
	suburb	13.7	21.3
Black		19.6	31.2
	central city	20.3	31.7
	suburb	18.8	30.0
Latino		16.5	27.7
	central city	16.0	28.9
	suburb	16.5	23.7
Total		15.7	24.6
	central city	16.4	25.9
	suburb	14.4	22.3

However, by definition, jobless durations are substantially longer than unemployment durations for each racial group in both areas. For example, central city black males' jobless durations are on average 11.4 weeks, or almost 3 months, longer than their unemployment durations, while white and Latino males' jobless durations are 7.8 and 12.9 weeks, respectively, longer than their unemployment durations. The longer jobless durations imply that the average unemployed person spends a considerable amount of time outside the labor force though still wanting to work. Since many individuals move directly from unemployment into employment, this evidence suggests that the remainder of those who withdraw from the labor force following an unemployment spell will experience significant periods of "hidden unemployment."

A much larger proportion of young black and Latino males experienced at least one bout of unemployment in 1984 than comparable whites in both the central city and suburbs. The following results suggest that most white male unemployment in both the central city and suburbs appears to be a result of a smaller proportion of the white male population suffering repeated, yet shorter unemployment spells than comparable black and Latino males in the same areas. Yet, whites' combined unemployment duration for each spell is still considerably shorter than that for black and Latino males. Black males' unemployment in both the central city and suburbs is the result of a larger part of their population suffering from less frequent, but much longer unemployment spells than comparable whites. Latinos' unemployment in the central city is the result of a larger part of their population, in comparison to central city whites, suffering from less frequent, but longer unemployment spells. However, when they live in the suburbs, their unemployment appears to be the result of a smaller part of their population, in comparison to their central city counterparts, suffering from more frequent, yet longer unemployment spells.

These results on unemployment dynamics suggest that residential location appears to matter for white males, but not for black males in metropolitan areas. Firm conclusions, however, cannot be made about the role of residential location without controlling for individual and metropolitan area characteristics, since both individual and metropolitan area differences could contribute to racial and residential location labor market differences. These results compliment Harrison's (1972) findings and offer little support for the spatial mismatch hypothesis of lower black employment. They also suggest that the spatial mismatch hypothesis may not have become more severe for certain low-skilled, young males since the 1960s. That is, it may have become worse for white males, whose labor market employment outcomes within metropolitan areas follows the standard urban model, but not for blacks.

Young white males have less labor market difficulties with respect to every facet of unemployment dynamics when they the live in the suburbs as opposed to the central cites, while young black males have severe labor market difficulties in either area. In fact, one could argue that young black males have more employment difficulties when they live in the suburbs as opposed to the central cities because of their higher suburban turnover and jobless rates. In addition, according to many of the unemployment indicators, they fall further behind their white counterparts when they live in the suburbs as opposed to the central cities. Although young Latino males have lower unemployment and jobless rates when they live in the suburbs than in central cities, their unemployment appears to be more concentrated when they live in the suburbs. Fewer young Latino males experience unemployment when they live in the suburbs as opposed to the central cities. However, those that do experience unemployment in the suburbs suffer longer durations and more frequent spells. Thus, for some young Latinos males, residence in the suburbs may improve their labor market outcomes, but for others, their labor market outcomes may get worse. Overall, however, their labor market position with respect to unemployment is better relative to whites when they live in suburbs versus the central cities. Some evidence is found, therefore, to suggest that young Latino males may experience labor market difficulties in metropolitan areas as a result of spatial mismatch.

The greater proportion of young black and Latino males experiencing at least one bout of unemployment contributes to observed racial youth unemployment differentials, by definition of the unemployment calculus. However, counter to intuition, young white males experience more spells on average than either black and Latino males in the central city and black males in the suburbs. The higher number of white males' spells of unemployment reduces racial differences in unemployment. In addition, although whites had more spells of unemployment than either blacks or Latinos, the combined average duration of these spells of unemployment is shorter than those of blacks and Latinos during the year. This suggests that spells of unemployment measure is not the proper unemployment dimension to use in examining racial differences in youth unemployment since spell differences between whites and blacks (Latinos) narrows the unemployment differences between these groups. In addition, the combined average duration measure for the year for each spell of unemployment is not the appropriate measure either for the same reason just mentioned. However, the unemployment duration measure is better to use in the analysis because blacks and Latinos problems are not continuous unemployment spells but rather long, uninterrupted spells.

Unemployment duration is significantly longer for young black and Latino males than for comparable whites in both the central city and suburbs. Cotton (1993) and Moore (1992) also find that unemployment duration is significantly longer for blacks than for comparable whites. It is reasonable to conclude, then, that longer unemployment durations of young black and Latino males contributes more to the racial youth unemployment differentials than spells of unemployment. In fact, Clark and Summers (1979), in their seminal article on unemployment dynamics, showed that unemployment duration is the most crucial component of observed unemployment rates of youth and adults alike. Before we examine the causes of racial unemployment duration differences, it seems a good idea to look deeper into the distribution and concentration of young males' unemployment durations in the central city and suburbs.

CONCENTRATION AND DISTRIBUTION OF JOBLESS SPELLS ACROSS RESIDENTIAL AREAS

In the previous section, I analyzed unemployment duration using the mean duration of an unemployment spell. However, as Clark and Summers (1979) have shown, unemployment duration can also be analyzed using the distribution of unemployment duration. The use of unemployment duration distributions allows one to calculate the fraction of total unemployment attributable to spells of different duration. In addition, unemployment duration distributions can reveal very different things about unemployment duration than can the mean. For example, if thirty spells of unemployment began lasting one week, and one spell of unemployment began lasting thirty weeks, the mean duration of an unemployment spell would be 1.9. However, the mean measure of unemployment duration could not convey the fact that one-half of the unemployment would be accounted for by the one spell that lasted thirty weeks. In this section, therefore, the distribution and concentration of unemployment and jobless durations for young males is analyzed to further examine whether residential location plays a role in the longer unemployment and jobless durations of black and Latino males.

Another issue of concern in examining unemployment dynamics is whether unemployment is seen as a temporary state experienced by many individuals as part of their normal job-search process, or what some have called "normal turnover" (Feldstein 1973), or as a relatively permanent state experienced by only a few individuals (Clark and Summers 1979). Previous research on young adults suggests that they have more spells of unemployment than adults, but that these spells are of shorter duration (Clark and Summers 1979). Table 3.4 shows the proportion of unemployment and jobless spells that end within one month. This table shows that contrary to the "normal turnover" hypothesis, and contrary to other findings on young adults' spells of unemployment, a small percentage of young males' spells of unemployment end within one month.

Table 3.4: Proportion of Unemployment and Jobless Spells Ending Within One Month by Race and Residential Location: 1984

		Unemployment	Jobless
White		29.0	13.4
	central city	26.6	13.3
	suburb	31.8	13.8
Black		18.7	8.5
	central city	18.8	8.2
	suburb	18.5	7.3
Latino		23.2	9.4
	central city	22.1	9.0
	suburb	24.7	12.1
Total		26.3	12.0
	central city	23.6	10.3
	suburb	30.0	12.3

Racial differences in the proportion of unemployment spells ending within one month in the central city and suburbs are of considerable importance. A higher percentage of young white males' spells of unemployment end within one month than those of either black or Latino males in either residential location. This finding is consistent with those in the previous section and suggest that, once unemployed, white males in either the central city or suburbs have an easier time finding employment than either black or Latino males.[11] However, suburban white males have a larger proportion of their unemployment spells end within one month than their central city counterparts, suggesting that their ability to get a job is easier in the suburbs than in the central cities. The same is true for Latino males, though the proportion of their suburban spells ending within one month is only slightly higher than that of their central city counterparts. However, the proportion of young black males' unemployment spells that end within one month is approximately the same in both the central city and suburbs, suggesting that they have a difficult time getting a job in either residential area.

This exercise was also conducted for jobless spells. Although the proportion of jobless spells ending within one month is about half that for unemployment spells for each racial group in both residential areas, the racial differences in the trends are the same as those for unemployment spells.[12] However, the proportion of young white males' jobless spells ending within one month in the suburbs is only slightly greater than that in the central city. This suggests that when the additional and unaccounted for unemployed are taken into account, young white males in the suburbs may not be that better off than their central city counterparts. In the case of black males, once the jobless factor is taken into account, their ability to get a job in a short period of time may be more difficult in the suburbs than in the central city.

The results in Table 3.4 imply that the bulk of young males' unemployment duration spells in both the central city and suburbs come from long spells that last at least 2 or more months. In addition, since young white males tend to have a higher proportion of their unemployment spells end within one month than either young black and Latino males in both the central city and suburbs, it is easy to predict that black and Latino males have more spells that last two or more months than comparable whites in both areas. Table 3.5 shows the proportion of unemployment by length of spell for young males living in the central city and suburbs. This table shows that a higher percentage of black and Latino males' unemployment, when compared to that of whites in the central city and suburbs, is attributable to unemployment spells lasting at least two months.[13] Moreover, a higher percentage of black and Latino males' unemployment is attributable to unemployment spells lasting at least six months. This shows that in both the central city and suburbs, black and Latino males' longer unemployment spells make up more of these groups' unemployment than they do for white males. These results support our earlier findings on unemployment duration that suggested that young black and Latino males' unemployment is much more intractable than that of comparable whites in both the central city and suburbs.

In the central cities, black males have a higher percentage of their unemployment made of longer unemployment spells than either comparable whites or Latinos. While 18.8 percent of young black males' unemployment spells ended within one month in 1984, nearly

Does Living in the Suburbs Really Make a Difference? 57

half of their unemployment was attributable to unemployment spells lasting at least six months! That is, of all black males in the central city who experience unemployment at any time during the year, nearly half (44.0) experienced six months or more of unemployment before terminating their spell. The comparable figure for whites and Latinos is 27.0 and 30.0 percent, respectively.

Table 3.5: Proportion of Unemployment[a] by Race and Residential Location: 1984

	White	Black	Latino	Total
In months				
Central Cities				
2 or more	.73	.82	.78	.77
3 or more	.54	.65	.57	.58
4 or more	.40	.57	.46	.46
5 or more	.31	.49	.34	.37
6 or more	.27	.44	.30	.32
Suburbs				
2 or more	.68	.81	.76	.70
3 or more	.52	.70	.66	.55
4 or more	.43	.58	.52	.47
5 or more	.36	.47	.43	.38
6 or more	.24	.35	.38	.26

[a] Expressed as a fraction of the total weeks of unemployment within the specific race/ethnicity-residential location categories.

The concentration of unemployment towards longer spells is not eased in the suburbs for young males, nor is the intensity of racial differences in these concentrations of longer spells. For young white males in the suburbs, the percent of all their unemployment attributable to spells lasting at least 4 or more and 5 or more months is greater than that in the central city. The same is also true for young Latino males. However, the percent of all black males' unemployment in the suburbs attributable to spells lasting 4 or more or 5 or more months is, in essence, the same as that in the central city. In all cases, except Latinos, the percentage of all unemployment attributable to spells lasting 6 or more months in the suburbs is less than in the central city.

A number of conclusions can be drawn from the data in Table 3.5. First, it is clear that young black and Latino males' unemployment in relation to that of comparable whites is more attributable to longer spells of unemployment in either the suburbs or central cities. However, living in the suburbs may, to some degree, ease the intractableness of unemployment for white and black, but not Latino males. Finally, these results also show that living in the suburbs does nothing to reduce the racial differences in the concentration of unemployment in longer spells.

Before we fully accept these conclusions, we must deal with the fact that spells of unemployment can end in either employment or withdrawal from the labor force. This fact has implications on how we interpret the completion of unemployment spells that we examined in the preceding two tables. If, for example, young males had the same percentage of their spells end within one month and that all their spells ended in employment, it would be tempting to conclude that there was no difference in young white, black, and Latino males' probability of getting a job, given that they were unemployed. However, if in fact one half of young blacks' and Latinos' unemployment spells ended in withdrawal while none did for whites, then the preceding inference would be wrong, since the data would now show that young blacks and Latinos were still without work even after their unemployment spells ended. Thus, it seems reasonable to find out whether there exists a racial difference in the ending of unemployment spells in employment to clarify whether our inferences based on the earlier two tables were indeed correct.

Table 3.6 shows the percentage of spells ending in either employment or withdrawal for young males in the central city and suburbs, irrespective of the month in which the spell ended. Slightly more unemployment spells end in employment in the suburbs as compared to the central cities. Following this trend, young white and Latino males' spells of unemployment are more likely to end in employment in the suburbs than in the central city. Conversely, their spells of unemployment are more likely to end in withdrawal in the central city than in the suburbs. However, these trends do not hold true for black males. Their spells of unemployment are more likely to end in withdrawal in the suburbs than in the central city. This result confirms are earlier suspicion that black males seem to have a harder time getting a job once unemployed in the suburbs than in the central city, while young white and Latino males appear to have an easier time. However, there is no clear reason why black workers get more discouraged and drop out of the labor force in the suburbs than in the central city. Table

3.6 also shows that young white males' spells of unemployment are more likely to end in employment in both the central city and suburb than comparable blacks and Latinos.

Table 3.6: Likelihood of Unemployment Spells Ending in Employment/Withdrawal by Race and Residential Location: 1984

	White	Black	Latino	Total
Central Cities				
Spells ending in employment	.66	.58	.62	.64
Spells ending in withdrawal	.34	.42	.38	.36
Suburbs				
Spells ending in employment	.69	.53	.64	.66
Spells ending in withdrawal	.31	.47	.36	.34

These results suggest that our inferences about racial differences in unemployment made from the previous two tables may be more true than the data lead us to believe. They also suggest that, as Clark and Summers (1979) pointed out, the unemployment duration of spells is an inadequate indicator of the ease or difficulty of finding work because of high exit rates from the labor force during unemployment spells. Thus, these results point to the importance of a using a jobless duration measure that includes the officially measured unemployed and those classified as not-in-the-labor-force, but who are able to work, in any study of unemployment since there may be little difference between these two labor market states. They also suggest that the racial differences in the likelihood of unemployment spells ending in employment have implications on how we interpret the distribution and concentration of unemployment spells. They suggest that young black and Latino males' unemployment may be more intractable than that of comparable whites even if their unemployment distributions are the same.

Another way to examine the concentration of unemployment and joblessness is to examine the distribution of unemployed and jobless persons and weeks. Table 3.7 shows the distribution of the unemployed and jobless for each racial group by residential location. Two main conclusions can be drawn. First, the pattern of unemployment and jobless concentrations is different for white than for comparable black and Latino males in both the central city and suburbs. Young white males' unemployment and joblessness, when compared to those of young black and Latino males, are much more concentrated in shorter spells in both areas. In the central city, 25.6 percent of the white male labor force who experienced three-and-a-half months of unemployment accounted for 65.0 percent of all the unemployment for this group. The comparable figures for young black and Latino males is 27.7 and 31.4 percent, respectively, and 47.3 and 60.3 percent, respectively. This same pattern also holds true for unemployment in the suburbs and for joblessness in both the central city and suburbs. Conversely, black and Latino males' unemployment is more concentrated in longer spells. In the suburbs, for example, the 13.3 and 12.2 percent of the black and Latino male labor force, respectively, who experienced over six months of unemployment accounted for 38.8 and 26.8 percent, respectively, of all unemployment for these groups. The comparable figures for young white males is 7.1 and 17.7 percent. Again, this same pattern holds for central city unemployment and for joblessness in both the central city and suburbs.

Second, residence in the suburbs does not substantially alter nor improve the concentration of unemployment or jobless for either young white, black and Latino males. In fact, whereas 38.8 of all joblessness for young suburban black males is attributable to its members who are out of work for more than six months, only 31.6 percent is for young central city black males. This suggests that young black male joblessness is more concentrated in longer spells in the suburbs than in the central city. This also confirms the results of the previous section in this chapter. However, Latinos' joblessness is less concentrated in longer spells in the suburbs than in the central city, suggesting that a suburban residence may improve their employment opportunities.

An examination into the distribution and concentration of unemployment and jobless spells confirms our earlier conclusions about whether residential location matters in the unemployment differences between young white and black (Latino) males. This examination shows that young black males experience longer and more concentrated unemployment and jobless spells than young white males in either the suburbs and central cities, and that no improvement is made by blacks in terms of easing their unemployment and joblessness

Table 3.7: Distribution of Unemployment and Joblessness by Race and Residential Location: 1984 (in weeks)

	White		Black		Latino		Total	
	Unemp.	Jobless	Unemp.	Jobless	Unemp.	Jobless	Unemp.	Jobless
	Unemployed and Jobless Persons (percent of labor force)							
Central Cities								
1–4	10.5	4.7	10.6	4.9	11.5	4.5	10.6	4.7
5–14	15.1	11.7	17.1	9.3	19.9	10.3	16.0	11.0
15–26	6.8	8.7	12.3	9.3	8.5	9.7	8.2	8.9
27–39	3.7	6.8	8.7	11.4	8.0	9.3	5.3	8.1
40+	3.4	7.5	9.9	23.8	4.3	18.5	4.9	12.3
Suburbs								
1–4	12.7	6.2	11.7	4.4	11.2	5.1	12.4	6.0
5–14	13.2	11.5	19.1	11.0	13.8	10.7	13.6	11.5
15–26	7.0	7.8	19.3	12.3	8.2	9.3	7.9	8.2
27–39	4.7	7.8	3.4	10.6	10.5	12.7	4.9	8.3
40+	2.4	6.7	9.9	24.8	1.7	7.6	2.9	8.0

Table 3.7 continued

	Weeks of Unemployment and Joblessness (percent of weeks)							
Central Cities								
1–4	26.6	12.0	18.1	8.3	22.1	8.5	23.6	10.5
5–14	38.4	29.7	29.2	15.9	38.2	19.8	35.6	24.5
15–26	17.2	22.0	21.0	15.8	16.2	18.6	18.3	19.8
27–39	9.5	17.3	14.8	19.4	15.3	17.8	11.7	17.9
40+	8.4	19.1	16.8	40.5	8.3	35.4	10.9	27.3
Suburbs								
1–4	31.8	15.4	18.5	7.0	24.7	11.3	30.0	14.3
5–14	33.0	28.9	30.2	17.5	30.5	23.5	32.6	27.4
15–26	17.5	19.5	30.5	19.4	18.1	20.4	18.8	19.6
27–39	11.7	19.5	19.7	16.8	23.1	27.9	11.7	19.7
40+	6.0	16.7	19.1	39.3	3.7	16.8	6.8	19.1

by living in the suburbs. It also shows that their unemployment difficulties are equally poor, and in some instances much worse, when they live in the suburbs as opposed to the central cities. This examination also shows that young Latino males, on the other hand, have less unemployment difficulties when they live in the suburbs as compared to the central cities, and that there relative position with respect to whites improves when they live in the suburbs as opposed to the central cities. Again, support is found for the spatial mismatch hypothesis in the case of young white males, and to a certain extent young Latino males, but not young black males.

CONCLUSION

In this chapter, I directly tested the spatial mismatch hypothesis by comparing the economic welfare of less-educated, out-of-school young males in the central city and suburbs using dynamic labor market outcome measures. The hypothesis suggests that suburban residents should perform better in the labor market than their central city counterparts. Little support for the hypothesis was found in the case of blacks since their labor market outcomes remained equally bad in the suburbs as in the central city. The most support for the hypothesis was found in the case of young white males. By most labor market indicators, they performed much better in suburbs than in central cities. As a result, for some labor market measures, blacks' and Latinos' outcomes were worse relative to those of whites in the suburbs than in the central city. The results imply that whites receive a bigger employment boost by having a suburban residential location, possibly suggesting that suburban labor market discrimination limits minority youth's access to suburban jobs.

These findings are consistent with those of Harrison (1972), and to a certain extent, Ellwood (1986). Harrison found that blacks, unlike whites, had worse labor market outcomes by certain labor market measures in the suburbs than in the central city. Ellwood found that in the West and South side of Chicago, areas with different job opportunities for youth, black youth had the same labor market outcomes. Furthermore, he found that in the West side where more job opportunities existed, white youth received the vast share of jobs. However, some researchers have noted and shown that the spatial mismatch may have become more pronounced over time since Harrison's study (Jencks and Mayer 1990). It is not entirely clear why the results in this chapter do not conform to these expectations. It could be due to the fact that, unlike Jencks and Mayer (1990), the sample was restricted to young males with limited schooling and used dynamic measures of labor market outcomes to investigate this issue. Furthermore, limiting the sample to young people minimizes the endogeneity problem of residential and job location and the problem of the selectivity of suburban residents. Ignoring these problems while using central city/suburban comparisons as a test of the spatial mismatch, as I noted in the previous chapter, will tend to overstate the effect of the spatial mismatch.

Another reason why spatial mismatch may not explain blacks' employment difficulties is that in using the central city/suburban comparison method as a test of the spatial mismatch, endogeneity bias still affects the overall results. Although this dataset is composed of young people, the majority of whom live at home, and as such whose residential location can be considered exogenous, the endogeneity problem is still at issue.[14] It is likely that many of these youth are unable to move out of the home precisely because of employment difficulties, thereby making their residential location less exogenous. However, the spatial mismatch effect tends to be overestimated when the endogeneity of residential location is not taken into account. But since efforts were made to minimize this bias, it is likely that the endogeneity issue here may not be that severe.

The biggest problem, however, in using central city/suburban comparisons to test the spatial mismatch hypothesis seems to be the inability to control for the residential patterns of black suburbanization. That is, blacks and Latinos who move to the suburbs could be relegated to that part of the suburbs that is more dilapidated, adjacent to the central city, and where jobs have left. If this is true, there may be little difference in the labor market opportunities facing suburban or central city blacks. Neglecting this facet of black suburbanization will tend to underestimate the effect of spatial mismatch. It is likely, then, that my inability to control for these suburbanization patterns by using a central city/suburban comparison of labor market outcomes across multiple metropolitan areas could be responsible for the results shown here. In chapter 5, we explore this issue in more depth with a case study of Washington, DC.

CHAPTER 4
The Impact of Job Movement from Central Cities to Suburbs on Young Men's Employment

As we learned in chapter 1, Kain's (1968) original theory of black unemployment is made of three distinct hypotheses: 1) that residential segregation determines the geography of black employment; 2) that residential segregation intensifies black unemployment; and 3) that the negative effect of residential segregation on black unemployment is intensified by job decentralization. This chapter examines the last of these hypotheses. In addition, the initial results from chapter 3 also suggest that race, or the way in which minority youth are treated in labor markets, also affects their ability to attain employment. Thus, in this chapter, I examine the relative importance of the movement of jobs from central cities to suburbs (i.e., job decentralization) and race as explanations of minority youth's employment problems. I contend that if the spatial mismatch hypothesis is a plausible explanation of racial differences in unemployment, it must affect those components of the unemployment rate for which racial differences are greatest. The results in chapter 3 indicate that of the components of the unemployment rate—spells, incidence, and duration—racial differences in duration are significant. Thus, jobless duration is used in this chapter as a key unemployment outcome measure in the analysis.

METROPOLITAN DISTRIBUTION OF JOBS AND PEOPLE AND DIMENSIONS OF YOUNG MEN'S JOBLESSNESS

The spatial mismatch between the location of jobs and the residences of blacks, and to a lesser extent Latinos, is a compelling explanation of racial differences in unemployment because of the extent to which jobs have moved from central cities to the suburbs over the last 20 years. Table 4.1 shows the concentration of jobs and people in the central cities of US metropolitan areas from 1970 to 1990. Panel A shows that jobs, irrespective of how they are defined, became more decentralized during this twenty year period, although the pace of decentralization was greater in the 1970s than the 1980s. This evidence seems to support the contention that central city employment opportunities have declined over time (Kasarda 1989; Wilson 1987). However, the decentralization of high-skill jobs was much more rapid than that of low-skill ones in the 1980s. Jobs in industries where the majority of youth work have decentralized at about the same rate as all jobs in both the 1970s and 1980s.

The spatial mismatch hypothesis suggests that residential location in the central city would be associated with greater employment difficulties given that jobs have moved and are moving from central cities to suburbs. Panel B shows that, for each year indicated, a greater percentage of blacks and Latinos than whites live in the central cities of metropolitan areas. Though blacks and Latinos have increasingly moved to the suburbs since the 1970s, housing market discrimination has largely kept blacks', and to a lesser extent Latinos', residential locations concentrated in the central city (Yinger 1995; Massey and Denton 1989). In addition, blacks who do move to the suburbs are largely restricted to those parts of the suburbs that border the central city (Kain, 1985). Thus, it is not altogether clear whether a suburban residential location for blacks improves their spatial access to jobs.

Given blacks' and Latinos' greater residential concentration in central cities, we should expect them to have worse labor market outcomes than their white counterparts if residential location matters in the way that the spatial mismatch hypothesis suggests. The first column of Table 4.2 shows the 1984 unemployment rate of young men in metropolitan areas. The young black and Latino male unemployment rate is 2.5 and 1.5 times, respectively, higher than that of their white counterparts. However, analysis of racial differences in unemployment rates tells us little about specific unemployment experiences that drive

Table 4.1: Percentage of Jobs and Population in Central Cities of US Metropolitan Areas, 1970–1990

	1970	1980	1990	%Change 70–80	%Change 80–90	%Change 70–90
A. Jobs						
All Jobs	57.3	53.0	52.3	-7.5	-1.3	-8.7
Low-Skill[a]	53.8	48.7	48.3	-9.5	-0.8	-10.2
High-Skill[b]	59.5	55.7	53.7	-6.7	-3.6	-9.7
Jobs in Industries Where Youth Work	55.2	51.0	50.3	-7.6	-1.4	-8.9
B. Population						
White	39.8	34.9	34.1	-12.3	-2.3	-14.3
Black	76.4	72.8	68.9	-4.7	-5.4	-9.8
Latino	62.0	60.3	57.0	-2.7	-5.5	-8.1
Total	45.2	42.1	40.4	-6.9	-4.0	-10.6

Source: 1970, 1980, 1990 *US Census*. Notes: All measures are weighted averages. [a]Includes jobs in craft, laborer, service, and farming occupations. [b]Includes jobs in managerial, professional, technical, sales, and clerical occupations. Includes only jobs in retail trade, service, and manufacturing industries.

these differences. As we discussed in chapter 3, the unemployment rate is made up of three distinct factors: 1) "incidence of unemployment", or the percentage of individuals who ever become unemployed sometime during the year; 2) "frequency", or the number of spells of unemployment the individual has during the year; and 3) "duration," or the time that a given spell of unemployment lasts, and is mathematically related to the unemployment rate shown by equation (3.1) in chapter 3.

Table 4.2: Dimensions of Young Males' (Aged 19 to 27) Unemployment by Race: 1984

	Unemployment Rate (%)	Duration (weeks)	Frequency (spell)	Incidence (%)
A. Levels				
White	10.0	14.5	1.42	25.2
Black	25.2	19.6	1.33	50.2
Latino	15.0	16.5	1.36	34.8
B. Ratios				
Black/White	2.52	1.35	0.94	1.99
Latino/White	1.50	1.14	0.96	1.38

Source: National Longitudinal Survey of Youth, 1984

Table 4.2 summarizes the dimensions of unemployment for young men. Analysis shows that duration and incidence of unemployment is the largest contributors to racial differences in unemployment rates. Young black and Latino males are nearly 99 and 38 percent, respectively, more likely than their white counterparts to ever experience a bout of unemployment during the year. In addition, racial differences in the duration of unemployment also contribute to racial differences in the unemployment rate. Young black and Latino males' duration of unemployment is about 5 and 2 weeks longer, respectively, than that of their white counterparts. On the other hand, racial differences in the unemployment rate are not generated by the frequency (spells) of unemployment because, conditional on experiencing unemployment, young white males are more likely than other groups to have bouts of unemployment. This suggests that for those who experience unemployment, young white males have a significantly lower "cost" of unemployment than either young black or Latino males because of their shorter durations of unemployment. If young white males quit, are laid off or fired from their jobs, their time to re-employment is shorter than other groups. Consequently, we use duration as the measure of unemployment in analyzing racial differences in unemployment.

DATA, EMPIRICAL MODEL, AND DEFINITIONS OF VARIABLES

I again use 1984 data from National Longitudinal Survey of Youth (NLSY) merged with data from the 1972 and 1982 *US Census of Industries* (1975, 1985) to examine the impact of job decentralization on young males' jobless durations.[15] I use data from 1984 because it was a post-recession year in which the economy operated at fairly high levels. The sample selection is defined the same as that described in the previous chapter.

To estimate the effect of job decentralization on the jobless durations of young men, I use Weibull regression analysis.[16] The following empirical model is specified:

D = *f*(Personal and Family Characteristics, Unemployment
Compensation, Local Unemployment Rate, Job Decentralization,
% of Central City (Suburban), % of Labor Force White (Black or
Latino), Total Population)   (4.1)

where D is equal to the length of the jobless duration. In these models, an independent variable that has a positive sign is positively related to jobless durations, i.e., associated with longer jobless durations. This positive sign also suggests that the hazard rate is negatively associated with jobless durations. This means that the rate at which individuals leave jobless states and enter employment increases when job decentralization decreases in metropolitan areas. In the duration equation, factors that I expect to be associated with shorter jobless durations, or higher hazard rates of leaving jobless states, include a low level of job decentralization,[17] and lower intensities of racial discrimination in the labor market as measured by competition from other racial groups in the labor force. If, for example, employers prefer whites over blacks, we should expect to find young white males' jobless duration decrease as the percentage of blacks in the labor force increases. If employers are predisposed to discriminate against minority youth, as the numbers of minorities grow in metropolitan areas, the opportunity to discriminate against them therefore increases. Conversely, we should expect to find a positive relationship between young black males' jobless duration and the percentage of whites in the labor force. The results are found on the coefficients for % of central city (suburb) that is white (black or Latino).

Other factors that I expect to be associated with shorter jobless durations include personal and family characteristics: being older (age), having more education, being married, having children. Also, I expect a lack of unemployment compensation receipt and a low unemployment rate in metropolitan areas to be related to shorter jobless durations. Unemployment income subsidizes the job search process so that duration may increase if individuals have unemployment compensation. However, most respondents in the sample did not receive unemployment compensation since to qualify for unemployment insurance a worker has to have been laid off from a previous job and to have worked a minimum amount of time. In this regard, then, receipt of unemployment insurance may actually shorten duration because, one, it may send a positive signal to employers about the worker, and, two, those who receive unemployment compensation may be the 'best' workers in the sample to search and find work. Thus, the effect of unemployment income is in fact an empirical question. The definition of these variables are shown in Table 4.3.

According to Kain (1968), the spatial mismatch hypothesis suggests that job decentralization negatively affects the economic welfare of blacks more than whites because of the role that residential segregation plays in limiting blacks' ability to follow jobs to the suburbs. However, it could also negatively affect the economic welfare of central city residents relative to their suburban counterparts, in general, if the former also face some kind of residential mobility constraint. Moreover, because blacks also tend to be residentially segregated in parts of suburban areas where jobs have also left, job decentralization may negatively effect their economic welfare as well (Holzer et al. 1994). Therefore, I show here separate regressions for young white, black, and Latinos males in the central cities and suburbs to investigate the differential affect of job decentralization on the jobless durations of these racial groups. In the final samples, young men represented 152 different central cities and 160 different suburbs.[18] Most of the central cities and suburbs in this sample, however, are a part of the same SMSA.

Table 4.3 : Definition of Variables
(Variables from 1985 NLSY unless otherwise noted)

Variable Name	Definition of Variables
Duration	Identifies the week during the 52 week year (1984) in which the jobless individual receives a job.
Work	Dummy variable equal to 1 if the jobless individual receives a job during the interview year (1984); 0 otherwise. Those with 0 are treated as censored in the hazard analysis.
Age	Age in years.
Highest Grade Completed	Completed years of education.
Married	Dummy variable equal to 1 if individual is married; 0 otherwise.
Children	Dummy variable equal to 1 if individual has children; 0 otherwise.
Unemployment Compensation	Dummy variable equal to 1 if individual is receiving unemployment compensation; 0 otherwise.
Local Unemployment Rate	Continuous unemployment rate for SMSA in which individual resides.
Job Decentralization	The percentage of all manufacturing, retail trade, and service jobs in an SMSA located in the suburbs. (1982 *US Census of Industries*.)

Table 4.3 continued

Variable Name	Definition of Variables
% of CC (SUB) L. F. White	The percentage of central city (suburban) residents in the labor force who are white. (1980 and 1990 *US Census*; extrapolations to 1984.)
% of CC (SUB) L. F. Black	The percentage of central city (suburban) residents in the labor force who are black. (1980 and 1990 *US Census*; extrapolations to 1984.)
% of CC (SUB) L. F. Latino	The percentage of central city (suburban) residents in the labor force who are Latino. (1980 and 1990 *US Census*; extrapolations to 1984.)
Total Population	Total SMSA population in which individual resides.

RESULTS OF JOBLESS DURATION MODELS

In the following sections, I report the results of models for central city and suburban residents. First, I briefly describe the summary statistics for young males. Secondly, I report the results of the duration equations while paying particular attention to the job decentralization and competing racial group variables. Finally, I discuss my findings and then conclude.

Central City Models

Descriptive Statistics

The means and standard deviations of the variables are presented in Table 4.4. The descriptive statistics confirm our results from chapter 3 and show that young white males have shorter jobless durations on average than either young black or Latino males, with young black males' durations being the longest. Also, a greater percentage of young white males receive jobs by the end of the year compared to their young black or Latino male counterparts. This latter result is interpreted from the variable "work". Young black males are more likely to live in central cities with greater job decentralization than either young white or Latino males. If job decentralization does in fact lengthen jobless durations, we might expect it to lengthen those of blacks much more than those of whites or Latinos. A greater percentage of young white and Latino males are married. Blacks live in central cities with smaller populations.

Table 4.4: Means (Std. dev.) for White, Black, and Latino Central City Models

Variable	White	Black	Latino
Duration	25.6	31.9	28.2
	(19.0)	(19.4)	(19.3)
Work	.76	.61	.70
	(.43)	(.49)	(.46)
Married	.21	.09	.23
	(.41)	(.29)	(.42)
Age	22.7	23.2	22.8
	(2.2)	(2.1)	(2.2)
Highewst Grade Completed	11.2	11.7	10.8
	(1.8)	(2.0)	(2.0)
Children	.21	.28	.24
	(.41)	(.45)	(.43)
Unemployment Compensation	.09	.07	.12
	(.29)	(.26)	(.32)
Local Unemployment Rate	9.2	9.0	9.1
	(2.9)	(2.9)	(3.6)
Job Decentralization	41.6	48.1	38.2
	(19.4)	(23.0)	(22.3)
% of CC Labor Force/White	—	50.6	50.7
		(16.2)	(15.3)
% of CC Labor Force/Black	20.3	—	17.4
	(16.0)		(13.1)
% of CC Labor Force/Latino	9.3	9.2	—
	(11.8)	(10.4)	
Total Pop. (log)	13.6	11.8	14.4
	(14.1)	(14.5)	(14.7)

Results of Central City Duration Models

Table 4.5 shows the results of the jobless duration equations for each racial group. The results show that the negative effect of job decentralization on jobless durations is statistically significant for blacks only.[19] These results are generally consistent with more recent studies of the effect of levels of job decentralization on employment

Table 4.5: Maximum Likelihood Weibull Estimates of Jobless Durations for Central City Young Males

Variable	White (1)	Black (2)	Latino (3)
Constant	3.823***	3.440***	-1.952
	(1.086)	(1.067)	(1.279)
Age	0.004	-0.034	-0.039
	(0.041)	(0.035)	(0.045)
Highest Grade Completed	0.033	0.121***	0.038
	(0.049)	(0.039)	(0.059)
Married	0.178	0.522***	-0.135
	(0.279)	(0.229)	(0.266)
Children	-0.489**	-0.050	0.290
	(0.240)	(0.172)	(0.216)
Unemployment Compensation	0.788**	0.912***	0.386
	(0.280)	(0.240)	(0.282)
Local Unemployment Rate	-0.019	-0.076***	-0.099***
	(0.031)	(0.024)	(0.032)
Job Decentralization	-0.002	-0.007**	-0.001
	(0.005)	(0.003)	(0.005)
% of CC Labor Force/White	—	-0.007**	-0.004
		(0.003)	(0.007)
% of CC Labor Force/Black	0.016***	—	-0.029
	(0.006)		(0.080)
% of CC Labor Force/Latino	0.004	0.000	—
	(0.008)	(0.008)	
Total Population (log)	0.001	0.002	0.001
	(0.004)	(0.005)	(0.006)
Log Likelihood	-293.49	-474.83	-235.23
Prob>chi2	0.00	0.00	0.00
N	174	242	121
Sigma	1.02	1.07	1.03

Notes: std. errors in parenthesis; * significant at .10, ** significant at .05, *** significant at .01.

and earnings (Holzer et al. 1994; Ihlanfeldt and Sjoquist 1989; Farley 1987) and suggest that the movement of jobs from central cities to suburbs negatively affects blacks' employment more than other groups. This is likely true because unlike whites, and to a lesser extent Latinos, blacks are unable to adjust their housing patterns to the shifting location of labor demand as a result of suburban housing market discrimination. Urban economic theory suggests that residential location is chosen by maximizing individuals who trade-off quality and cost of housing with the length and burden of commutes to work. In our case, a housing choice in the suburbs for low-skill workers makes sense because housing in the suburbs gets you more house for your money and because job growth is more substantial there. Thus, commutes by suburban residents to suburban jobs are likely manageable. The insignificant coefficient estimate for whites and Latinos for the effect of job decentralization on duration suggests that these groups likely live in households where housing choices have been made to bring their work-housing trade-off into equilibrium. The significant and positive coefficient for blacks suggest that barriers exist in either the housing or labor market that do not allow such equilibrium to take place for this group. These barriers are likely found in the housing market, which prevent blacks from moving to the suburbs to take advantage of the growing job opportunities there.

The effect of one or both of the competing racial groups in the labor force variables is significant in the white and black models, but not the Latino one. The positive and significant coefficient for % of CC L.F.-Black variable in the white equation means that as the percentage of blacks in the labor force who live in the central city increases, the jobless durations of young white males in the central city decreases. This implies that employer discrimination against blacks in the central city leads to an employment premium for whites. Furthermore, this effect for whites is strong enough to offset the negative effect of job decentralization on their jobless durations. Farley (1987) and Dowdall (1974) have shown that whites are generally better-off in relation to blacks the larger the size of the black population in the area. They argue that this is true because as the number of blacks increases in cities, the opportunity to discriminate by whites goes up. Thus, whites are better able to gain jobs and income by using racial discrimination to reserve better jobs for themselves. However, this assumes that employees and not employers are in a position to discriminate. While this is contested terrain, it is not unreasonable to believe that whites, particularly if they are the dominant group in the city, can apply pressure on employers to discriminate. However, their ability to apply such pressure on employers to discriminate may decrease as blacks become the dominant group in the city.

To test Farley's (1987) and Dowdall's (1974) hypothesis that whites are better off in labor markets given an increasing black presence, I split the variable % of CC L.F.-Black in the white model into 5 dummy variables representing different levels of black presence in central city labor markets. I then re-ran the Weibull equation for whites, substituting these dummy variables for the continuous % of CC L.F.-Black variable. I used the middle or 3rd dummy variable, defined as blacks making up 20 to 35 percent of the central city labor force, as the reference variable. The results and the cutoff levels for the dummy variables are shown in the appendix, Table A4.3.

If Farley's and Dowdall's hypothesis is correct, then we should expect both dummy variables representing higher concentrations of blacks in the central city labor force to be significant and positive in the equation. These expected results would suggest that as blacks become more of a threat to whites in the labor market as a result of their increasing presence in the central city, whites would adopt measures that would ensure limited competition for jobs from blacks. More precisely, this means that shorter jobless durations for whites would be associated with higher black presence in the central city labor force. The results show that this scenario is true only when blacks make up a fairly substantial part of the central city's labor force, i.e., 35 to 50 percent. The results of this dummy variables is very strong, .465, and significant, suggesting that whites' jobless durations are shorter given this level of black presence in the central city labor force.

However, if blacks represent a majority of the central city's labor force, white's jobless durations are not associated with blacks' presence in the labor market, since the coefficient on this dummy variable is insignificant and smaller in magnitude. This suggest that whites' ability or desire to limit competition for jobs is contingent on the concentration of blacks in the central city labor force. That is, when blacks represent a very small part of the central city's labor force, whites do not view them as a threat. However, when blacks represent a fairly large fraction of the central city's labor force, they might perceive blacks as a threat to employment and may adopt measures to limit competition for jobs. When blacks represent a majority of the central city's labor force, however, whites are likely unable to successfully adopt measures to limit competition for jobs because of blacks' greater ability to put pressure on employers to hire blacks. Thus, contrary to Farley's and Dowdall's hypothesis, there is a central city black presence threshold below which whites are able to successfully limit competition for jobs, and above which blacks are able to neutralize such measures by whites. This story refers mainly to employee driven discrimination, but the results just discussed are also consistent with consumer discrimination on the part of whites. That is, when there are few blacks in the central city, white consumers may not be inclined to pressure employers to not hire blacks. However, as the percentage of blacks increase in the central city, whites might be inclined to pressure employers not to hire blacks. This pressure can be applied by essentially boycotting stores that hire blacks, thereby causing employers to let go of, or refuse to hire, blacks in order to regain their customer base. When blacks represent the majority of the central city's labor force, they are also more likely to make up the majority of the consumers. In this case, blacks are less likely to boycott stores that hire blacks and their sheer numbers would also negate whites' attempts to do the same.

Conversely, the negative and significant coefficient for % of CC L.F.-White variable in the black equation suggests that there may be limited pure competition for jobs between blacks and whites in the central city. This implies that whites are preferred by employers, confirming the results in the white equation. Given these model's results, it is clear that race, or how blacks are treated in the labor market (and Latinos in the housing market), appears to be important in determining their longer jobless durations.

More support for this conclusion is offered by the results of the unemployment rate's effect on blacks' and Latinos' jobless durations. There is a tremendous literature that has shown youth unemployment rates to get worse during loose labor markets, or high unemployment rates, and better during tight labor markets (Freeman 1989). However, little research has examined these affects on young adult jobless durations. Acs and Wissoker (1991) and Lynch (1988), both using the NLSY, find that SMSA wide unemployment rates have substantial effects on the duration of spells of joblessness for central city residents and metropolitan residents, respectively. The large and significant effect of the unemployment rate on young black and Latino males jobless durations implies that as the unemployment rate increases their jobless durations increase significantly. This finding is consistent with previous research on durations and, in conjunction with the insignificant unemployment rate coefficient for whites, is also consistent with the idea that blacks and Latinos are less preferred by employers in central city labor markets, or what is commonly referred to as the first fired, last hired syndrome. In a similar vein, Mooney (1969) finds that the unemployment rate effect is stronger than the job decentralization effect in explaining higher black unemployment in relation to that of whites in the central city, suggesting, once again, that blacks' employment opportunities lag behind those of whites in the central city.

These results, however, also suggest that young black and Latino males do respond to the level of unemployment or demand, contradicting those who suggest that their unemployment difficulties are intractable and due primarily to supply-side factors such as their high reservation wage which contributes to their lack of motivation to work (Anderson 1980).

As noted, the unemployment rate is not associated with young white males' durations. Perhaps the effect of job decentralization is incorporating or dominating the effect of the unemployment rate. Since the unemployment rate effect is significant and negative on blacks' and Latinos' re-employment probability, and since running the black and Latino models with only one of these variables did not change their results, this possibility is unlikely. Therefore, it seems as though young white males' jobless durations are associated more with other factors than with the absolute tightness or looseness of the labor market. Conversely, for young black and Latino males, the overall tightness or looseness of the labor market is much more important than the spatial distribution of particular jobs. This result is also consistent with the idea that employer preferences for whites in the labor market buffers the negative effects of a high unemployment rate on their ability to get jobs.

The remaining significant variables are individual and could also lengthen or shorten young males' jobless durations. The receipt of unemployment compensation is positive for all three groups, but its magnitude is largest for blacks and whites. The positive sign for unemployment compensation in these models is rather interesting. Search theory suggests that the receipt of unemployment compensation will tend to increase the reservation wage of an unemployed worker. The receipt of unemployment compensation, then, should have a negative effect on duration of unemployment, or, more precisely, will tend to lengthen an unemployment spell. However, the positive sign on this variable for all groups suggests that the receipt of unemployment compensation may in fact be sending a positive signal to employers thereby raising the probability of receiving a job offer and shortening jobless durations. In order to receive unemployment compensation, a worker must have been laid off of a previous job and must have worked a minimum amount of time on that job. Employers may be using unemployment compensation, then, in their evaluation of young workers as a positive signal of productivity. In fact, Lynch (1988), using 1982 NLSY data, found unemployment compensation receipt to shorten youth's jobless durations as well. However, it is also likely that because one needs to be employed with a firm or company for a number of months before one receives unemployment compensation, the significance of this variable suggests that it is those who have had success in the labor market in the past that are most likely to get rehired elsewhere.

The larger magnitude of blacks' unemployment compensation coefficient in comparison to that of whites and Latinos is interesting and suggests that their characteristics are examined more carefully than those of whites and Latinos. If employers are unsure of the productivity or trainability of workers, they may be more inclined to use signals such as education, credentials, or even superficial characteristics such as race or ethnicity to discriminate against potential employees. If employers are more reluctant to hire blacks than either whites or Latinos because they associate blacks with low-skill or untrainability (Kirschenman and Neckerman 1991), then we should expect employers to scrutinize blacks' credentials and characteristics more than those of other groups. If employers view unemployment compensation receipt as a positive signal of stability, they may place more weight on unemployment compensation receipt for blacks, about whom they may be more unsure, than whites or Latinos.

Employers may also use educational attainment in the same way as they appear to use unemployment compensation. Unlike the white and Latino male models, the coefficient for highest grade completed is significant and positive in the black models. Each additional year of education for young black males in the central city decreases their jobless duration. It would be tempting to argue that jobless durations are shorter for more educated workers because, according to human capital theory, education increases productivity thus making educated workers more attractive to employers in the labor market (Becker

1964). It could also be argued that more education provides workers with more knowledge on how and where to search for work thereby shortening jobless durations. But since this variable is insignificant in the young white male models, it is difficult to accept this hypothesis, particularly when white workers have more education on average than their black and Latino counterparts in the central city. Given the results of the other variables, it seems more plausible that employers use education, as they do unemployment compensation, as a signal for productivity (or trainability), or, more precisely, as a screening device when hiring. This practice may be used more extensively for young black than either white or Latino males. Thurow (1978) argues that education is a signal to employers that workers have "industrial discipline." That is, having gone through the educational process, a worker demonstrates an ability to show up on time, take orders, and observe certain norms of group behavior that are fundamental to the work process and that contribute to productivity. Employers may be more hesitant to employ young black males without some tangible insurance that they may be a productive or trainable worker. The converse of this story, however, is that young black males in the job market with limited education are more likely to be turned away by employers than either whites or Latinos with similar educational characterisitcs.

Marriage is associated with shorter jobless durations for young black males in the central city suggesting that marriage causes them to either search more intensively for employment or lower their reservation wage thereby making more low-wage jobs available to them. However, marriage lengthens Latinos' jobless durations as does age. The first result suggests that perhaps more Latino male spouses work, thereby providing an alternative source of income, which allows them to extend their search time without significant cost. Finally, having children is associated with longer jobless durations for whites, suggesting that white males may have more child care responsibilities. These responsibilities compete with the search for work, contributing to longer jobless durations.

Suburban Models

We learned in chapter 3 that young blacks' and Latinos' jobless durations are longer than those of comparable whites in the suburbs as well. It seems reasonable, then, to explore the factors associated with these racial jobless duration differences as we did for the central city residents. As noted earlier, job decentralization should positively affect the economic welfare of suburban residents. However, Holzer et al. (1994) show that job decentralization also negatively affects the unemployment duration of young black suburban residents. They argue that because blacks tend to be re-segregated in parts of suburbs that are older, dilapidated, and usually directly adjacent to central cities, they still remain far removed from the suburban locus of jobs. For example, Ihlanfeldt (1992) notes that although blacks have begun to move to the suburbs of Atlanta, they have moved to the Southern suburbs located on the fringe of the central city ghetto where little job growth has occurred, and not the Northern suburbs where most of the job growth in Atlanta has located. These suburban re-segregation patterns for blacks may be responsible for the insignificant differences their unemployment outcomes in the central city and suburbs that we observed in chapter 3. In this section, suburban models of jobless duration are estimated to explore this issue and other factors that might explain blacks' longer jobless duration in the suburbs.

Descriptive Statistics

The means and standard deviations of the variables are presented in Table 4.6. The definitions of all variables are found in Table 4.3. The descriptive statistics confirm again that even in the suburbs young white males have shorter jobless durations on average than either their black or Latino counterparts, with black males' durations the longest. Also, like central city residents, a greater percentage of suburban white males received jobs by the end of the interview date compared to their black or Latino counterparts.

Young blacks and Latinos are more likely to live in suburbs with less job decentralization than their white counterparts. This means that suburban whites live in suburbs where jobs are more concentrated in the suburbs than in the central city, while blacks and Latinos are more likely to live in suburbs where jobs are more concentrated in the central city. A greater percentage of white and Latino males are married.

Table 4.6: Means (std. dev.) for White, Black, and Latino Suburban Models

Variable	White	Black	Latino
Duration	23.0	32.1	24.4
	(18.0)	(19.2)	(18.5)
Work	.82	.62	.79
	(.39)	(.49)	(.41)
Married	.28	.11	.28
	(.45)	(.32)	(.45)
Age	23.1	23.2	23.3
	(2.3)	(2.3)	(2.3)
Highest Grade Completed	11.5	11.4	11.1
	(1.5)	(1.6)	(1.9)
Children	.19	.31	.27
	(.39)	(.46)	(.45)
Unemployment Compensation	.12	.08	.13
	(.32)	(.27)	(.34)
Local Unemployment Rate	9.9	9.1	10.0
	(3.0)	(2.9)	(4.3)
Job Decentralization	50.3	45.3	40.2
	(18.8)	(22.1)	(21.7)
% of SUB Labor Force/White	—	80.3	66.7
		(15.1)	(20.8)
% of SUB Labor Force/Black	5.5	—	4.3
	(4.7)		(3.9)
% of SUB Labor Force/Latino	4.2	6.6	—
	(7.2)	(10.5)	
Total Population (log)	13.7	13.9	13.9
	(14.1)	(14.4)	(14.3)

Results of Suburban Duration Models

Table 4.7 shows the results of the suburban jobless duration equations for each racial group. All of the models are statistically significant. The results of the job decentralization variable are interesting. Note that the effect of growth in job decentralization is large in magnitude and

Table 4.7: Maximum Likelihood Weibull Estimates of Jobless Durations for Suburban Young Males

Variable	White (1)	Black (2)	Latino (3)
Constant	-6.900***	-3.601***	-2.889
	(1.230)	(1.209)	(1.252)
Age	0.032	-0.005	-0.002
	(0.037)	(0.038)	(0.041)
Highest Grade Completed	0.260***	0.115*	0.034
	(0.070)	(0.061)	(0.054)
Married	0.093	0.128	0.091
	(0.270)	(0.259)	(0.269)
Children	0.016	-0.302*	0.206
	(0.270)	(0.187)	(0.225)
Unemployment Compensation	0.398	0.666***	0.517**
	(0.252)	(0.267)	(0.265)
Local Unemployment Rate	-0.049	-0.120***	-0.063***
	(0.030)	(0.031)	(0.023)
Job Decentralization	-0.005	-0.012***	0.002
	(0.005)	(0.004)	(0.005)
% of SUB Labor Force/White	—	-0.007**	-0.006
		(0.003)	(0.006)
% of SUB Labor Force/Black	0.008**	—	-0.041
	(0.003)		(0.030)
% of SUB Labor Force/Latino	0.004	-0.015	—
	(0.003)	(0.011)	
Total Population (log)	0.001	0.002	0.000
	(0.006)	(0.005)	(0.001)
Log Likelihood	-265.63	-342.18	-239.40
Prob>chi2	0.00	0.00	0.04
N	179	117	62
Sigma	0.95	1.01	0.99

Notes: std. errors in parenthesis; * significant at .10, ** significant at .05, *** significant at .01.

statistically significant for suburban blacks. This result is consistent with findings in Holzer et al. (1994) and suggests, as Kain (1985) has shown, that many suburban blacks also have low spatial access to jobs because they tend to live in suburban areas that border the inner-city, are experiencing economic decline and are located far from outer-suburban job growth areas. Thus, this result suggests that we need be cautious in interpreting the results from chapter 3 which showed that blacks were equally likely to perform badly in the central city and suburban labor markets. The results from this caste doubt on the ability of the spatial mismatch hypothesis to explain blacks' low level of employment. To the extent that blacks live in suburban areas that are near inner city areas and that are themselves in economic depression, comparisons of the labor market performance of blacks who live in the central city and suburbs will likely bias the results against the spatial mismatch hypothesis.

Like the central city models, the effect of competing racial groups in the labor force is significant in the white and black models, but not the Latinos one. The positive and significant coefficient for the % of SUB L.F.-Black variable in the white equation means that as the percentage of blacks in the labor force who live in the suburbs increases, the jobless durations of young white males in the suburbs decreases. This implies, as it did in the central city models, that employer discrimination against blacks leads to an employment premium for whites in the suburbs as well. However, the effect is not as strong as the one in the central city model.

Like the central city models, I split the % of SUB L.F.-Black variable into dummy variables to examine whether and at what level of blacks presence in the suburbs do whites receive employment benefits on account of discrimination against blacks. Since blacks do not represent a majority of any suburb included in the analysis, and since the upper limit of the % of SUB L.F.-Black variable is only .346, I split the variable into 3 categories, using the middle category as the reference variable. While I do not show the results of this exercise, whites' jobless durations are significantly shorter when blacks represent between 20.0 and 34.6 percent of the suburban labor force, and are not significantly shorter when blacks represent between 0 and 10.0 percent. Whites' therefore either perceive blacks as a threat to their employment opportunities or pressure employers to discriminate against blacks through consumer tastes when blacks make up a fairly large fraction of the suburban population. However, it is not unreasonable to assume that if blacks became the numerical majority in some suburbs, that such discrimination might not take place either because blacks can apply pressure to suburban employers to hire more blacks or because consumer discrimination against blacks under these circumstances seems unlikely.

On the other hand, the negative and significant coefficient for % of SUB L.F.-White variable in the black equation suggests, as it did in the central city model, that there may be limited pure competition for jobs between blacks and whites in the suburbs. According to the model's results, whites appear to be preferred by employers. Again, race is an important factor in the labor market that negatively affects the jobless durations of black males.

Like the central city models, the importance of race is also confirmed by the results of the unemployment rate's effect on blacks' and Latinos' jobless durations. The large and significant effect of the unemployment rate on young black and Latino males jobless durations implies that as the unemployment rate increases their jobless durations increase as well. However, the unemployment rate effect on blacks' jobless durations is more than twice as strong as that for Latinos. These findings, nonetheless, are consistent with the idea that blacks and Latinos are less preferred than whites by employers in suburban labor markets.

The remaining significant variables are individual but could also lengthen or shorten young males' jobless durations. The receipt of unemployment compensation in these suburban models is only significant for blacks and Latinos, though the coefficient in the black model is larger than the one in the Latino model. Like the central city models, its sign is positive. The positive sign suggests, as it did in the central city models, that the receipt of unemployment compensation may in fact be sending a positive signal to employers thereby raising the probability of receiving a job offer and shortening the jobless duration, or it may simply reflect the endogeneity bias mentioned earlier. On the one hand, employers may be using unemployment compensation, then, in their evaluation of young workers as a positive signal of productivity. On the other hand, since to receive unemployment compensation individuals must have worked for a certain lentgh of time, its effect may simply be identifying individuals who are eager and consistent workers and who will do well in the labor market regardless.

Unlike the young Latino male model, the coefficient for highest grade completed is significant and positive in the white and black models. Each additional year of education for these groups decreases their jobless duration. However, the magnitude of the highest grade completed coefficient in the white model is over twice as large as the one in the black model. This is particularly interesting since this variable's coefficient was not significant in the white model for central city residents. The significance of this variable in the white model for the suburbs may stem from the fact that whites make up the clear majority of residents there. The employment premium that white males may receive in the central city because of employer discrimination against blacks and Latinos is not as great in the suburbs. This is likely true not because suburban employers do not engage in discriminatory behavior, but because blacks and Latinos make up so few of the suburban population. Therefore, fewer whites receive an employment premium as a result of discrimination. With more whites competing with each other for jobs in the suburbs, employers may be more inclined to distinguish between potentially "good" and "bad" white employees. Thus, jobless durations are shorter for more educated workers because, according to human capital theory, education increases productivity thus making educated workers more attractive to employers in the labor market (Becker, 1964). Employers may use education, then, as a signal for productivity (or trainability), or, more precisely, as a screening device when hiring, and this practice may have a more noticeable affect on the white model's coefficients in the suburbs since there is more competition there among whites for jobs.

Finally, having children is associated with longer jobless durations for blacks in the suburbs. The expectation was that young males would be more inclined to increase their search intensity for work or lower their reservation wage to provide for their children. However, the negative and fairly large coefficient on the children variable in the black suburban model suggests that black males may spend more time with child care responsibilities and that this activity may compete with the job search process, thereby lengthening their jobless duration.

CONCLUSION

The results in this chapter confirm the third proposition in Kain's (1968) original theory of black unemployment, that the negative effect of residential segregation on black unemployment is intensified by job decentralization. Unlike white and Latino men, young black men in both the central cities and suburbs are negatively affected by the extent of job decentralization in metropolitan areas. This suggests that blacks are unable to adjust their residential locations to adapt to the shifting location of employment demand due to housing market discrimination in areas where such jobs have located. However, suburban blacks are not unaffected by housing segregation. They too are negatively affected by such job decentralization suggesting that they likely live in suburban areas that are close to and resemble in economic condition the central city areas in which other blacks live. These results suggest that the interpretation of results in chapter 3 must be made with caution. To the extent that suburban blacks' residential locations are no different than their central city counterparts, we should expect to find little or no difference between the labor market outcomes of central city and suburban blacks. To the extent that this is true, we cannot conclude that the spatial mismatch of jobs and residences is not responsible for blacks' low level of employment. The results shown in this chapter therefore begs that we control for blacks' residential patterns in the suburbs before we conclude either way the effect of the spatial mismatch on blacks' employment. We do this in the next chapter.

The results of the following analysis also suggests that race, or how minorities are treated in the labor market, is an important determinant of their jobless problems as well. If racial discrimination in hiring is a pervasive problem in the labor market, then the lack of jobs available to blacks and Latinos caused by this discrimination is likely magnified by the extent of job decentralization. The impact of race on the employment of blacks, and to a lesser extent Latinos, appears to come in the form of a racialized labor queue. According to the analysis, it seems as though the extent of this racialized labor queue is conditional on two important factors, namely the level of aggregate demand and the percentage of blacks in a particular area. If the level of aggregate demand for employment is low as measured by a high unemployment rate, then there are fewer jobs to go around. Under this condition, whites may be more inclined to adopt measures to limit competition for these jobs if they are the numerical dominant group in a particular area. In this case, discrimination in any form, i.e., employee, employer, or consumer discrimination, against blacks in the labor market might become more intense. The practice of statistical discrimination might become more intense also since employers have more workers to chose from in hiring.

Second, if the presence of blacks in an particular area is high but not high enough to make them a numerically dominant group, then discrimination against blacks might also become more intense. Under these conditions, a more defined racial labor queue might emerge. It could also be true that the combination of these two conditions, namely limited jobs and a significant black presence in a particular area, might further contribute to the emergence of a racial labor queue.

Given that these structural factors could give rise to a racial labor queue in metropolitan areas, what might be the institutional mechanism that could produce such a queue? Thurow (1975) provides a theoretical model of a simple labor queue that could help us understand how a racial labor queue can take form. According to Thurow, individuals compete against one another for job opportunities based on their relative costs of being trained to fill whatever job is being considered. Most cognitive skills for particular jobs are not acquired before a worker enters the labor market, he argues, but only after the worker has found employment. Seen in this light, the labor market is primarily a training market, and not a bidding market for selling existing skills, as many economists argue, where training slots must be allocated to different workers.

Furthermore, this distribution of training slots and the allocation of individuals among these slots depend on two sets of factors. The first set includes the individual's relative position in the labor queue and the second includes the distribution of job opportunities in the economy. In Thurow's model, wages are paid based on the characteristics of the job in question and not the workers' skills, and workers are distributed across job (or training) opportunities based on their relative position in the labor queue. Workers compete for position in the queue based upon their background characteristics rather than on their willingness to accept low wages. Thus, the most preferred workers, or those with the most favorable background characteristics according to employers, get jobs first. Moreover, the least preferred workers get jobs when job opportunities in the economy expand.

According to Thurow, all workers possess background characteristics that employers evaluate, which, in turn, determines their position in the labor queue. These background characteristics include education, innate abilities, age, sex, personal habits, etc. In addition, these distinct characteristics affect the cost of training a worker to fill any job. Because of differences in background characteristics, each individual will have a different structure of associated training costs.

The problem for an employer is to pick and train workers to get the most marginal product as possible with the least investment in training costs. Training costs, as the term is used in Thurow's model, include "the costs of inculcating norms of industrial discipline, good work habits, and the uncertainty costs associated with hiring workers whose training costs are more variable or unknown" (Thurow 1975: 87). To minimize training costs, employers rank potential workers on the basis of their training costs. Moreover, this rank ordering of workers leads to the labor queue.

The results of the analysis in this chapter suggest that race is also an important background characteristic that employers consider in the hiring of workers as well. If employers are uncertain about the potential training costs of workers, about whose background characteristics they are uncertain as well, they will likely look more critically at indicators of trainability. The fact that the effects of education and unemployment compensation receipt is more powerful in the young black than white male equations for the central city suggests that employers scrutinize black males' characteristics more carefully than they do those of whites.

Although the analysis suggest that race is an important factor in hiring, the models designed here are not a direct test of discrimination in the labor market. However, using employer based interviews, Moss and Tilly (1993) find that employers are increasingly relying on race as an indicator of trainability in hiring, particularly as the kind of skills needed to perform work are changing in industries that hire youth. They suggest that the requirements for jobs in industries that employ many young adults, namely, manufacturing, retail trade and service, are changing to a set of "soft" skills. Based on their interviews with Los Angeles and Detroit area employers in manufacturing, retail trade, insurance companies, and the public sector, Moss and Tilly (1993) define these "soft" skills as "employees verbal skills, communication and people skills, teamwork skills, demeanor, flexibility, initiative, and general aspects of work attitudes and effort as opposed to "hard" skills such as literacy, computations, computer knowledge" (Moss and Tilly 1993: 2).

The nature of these changing job skill requirements are important, then, to understand the associated training costs of, and the kinds of background characteristics of workers needed to fill, these jobs. Moss and Tilly (1993) report that employers find that they can train anyone to perform the kinds of jobs offered, as Thurow suggests, but that these costs are minimized by workers possessing the right background characteristics. Moreover, these background characteristics are closely confounded with race. Thus, employers look critically at potential workers' appearance, speech, and demeanor, among other things. Employers see young black men as deficient in the background characteristics that they define as important in making up the "soft" skills needed to perform jobs effectively. Thus, employers are becoming more reluctant to hire young black men, Moss and Tilly argue, because they fear the associated costs of training black workers whom they feel will possess "bad" background characteristics will be too high. This is consistent with the results of the competing group variables in this analysis. This story is also consistent with the results of unemployment: the local unemployment rate has no effect on young white males' jobless durations while it lengthens the jobless durations of young black and Latino males. This suggests that employers prefer to hire young white males if they can. With sufficient numbers of young black and Latino males in the central city to shoulder the brunt of unemployment, young white males are essentially protected against fluctuations in the unemployment rate.

Further evidence of employers avoidance of young black workers in jobs that require these kinds of skills comes from the work of Kirschenman and Neckerman (1991). Based upon interviews with employers in the central city of Chicago and its surrounding suburbs, they find that employers use race as a primary distinction while making recruiting, screening and hiring decisions. They also argue that employers use negative racial stereotypes in conjunction with stereotypes of class and space (or residential location) to discriminate, statistically in most cases, against blacks, Puerto Ricans, and to some extent Mexicans-Americans. Thus, employers use race, class and residential location as barometers of whether workers have the necessary background characteristics to perform "soft" skill jobs. Kirschenman and Neckerman also find that the particular combination of background characteristics that matter to employers vary according to the demands and industry of the job. For example, employers in industries such as retail trade that require more employee-customer contact look for and hire workers with social interaction and communication skills, and that have a certain appearance. Their work suggests that racial stereotypes could be confused with perceived job related attributes such as communication skills, demeanor, dress, personality and initiative.

The results of the analysis shown here suggest that both race and space are important determinants of blacks', and to a lesser extent Latinos', low levels of employment in metropolitan areas. However, it is unclear which of these two factors are more important. We attempt to determine their relative importance in the next chapter.

CHAPTER 5
The Confounding Influence of Race in Space:
The Effect of Race and Residential Location on the Employment of Young Men in the Washington, DC Area

We have learned from earlier discussions that the spatial mismatch hypothesis attempts to explain blacks', and to some extent Latinos', worse labor market performances relative to those of whites in metropolitan areas as a consequence of their inability to follow jobs to the suburbs due to housing discrimination practices. The hypothesis suggests, therefore, that blacks and Latinos who move to the suburbs, controlling for the selectivity of movers and for the endogeneity problems of residential and job location, should perform better in the labor market than their central city counterparts.

In chapter 3, we found that while white and Latino youth had considerably better labor market outcomes in suburbs than in central cities, such was not the case for blacks. In fact, we found little or no differences in the their labor market outcomes between the central city and suburbs. However, we learned in the previous chapters that we could not conclude whether this evidence contradicted the spatial mismatch hypothesis because we did not control adequately for the suburban residential patterns of blacks. In chapter 3, the data we used to compare the labor market outcomes of central city and suburban residents came from well over 100 metropolitan areas. To the extent that blacks are segregated in suburban areas that are close to inner city areas and that are themselves in economic decline and with out jobs, we would likely find little or no differences in blacks' labor market outcomes between the central city and suburbs. Thus, in order to make reasonable conclusions about the spatial mismatch hypothesis when comparing central city and suburban employment outcomes, one must take into account such suburban residential patterns of blacks.

In addition, we also found in the previous chapter that race appeared to be a substantial factor in limiting the employment opportunities of minority youth. However, we were unable to determine whether race was as or more important than space in determining the lower employment rates of blacks, or whether the increasing intensity of racial discrimination as one moved from central city to suburbs limited the potential employment gains to be realized by blacks as a result of living in job-rich suburbs. As we noted earlier, if race becomes more important in the hiring of blacks in the suburbs than the central city, it is difficult to determine whether the lower employment of blacks is indeed a problem of their distance from jobs or a reflection of the problem of race in labor markets.

In this chapter, I use data from the Washington, DC metropolitan area to explore in more systematic detail the relative importance of race and space (residential location), and their possible interactions, in understanding racial employment differences for male youth. I have chosen the Washington, DC area because of the rapid black, and to some extent Latino, suburbanization that has taken place in Prince George's County, MD and because the area in Prince George's County where blacks have moved to is the same area where the majority of the county jobs are located and where most of the county job growth has occurred. Thus, by using the Washington, DC case study, we can control for the suburban residential patterns of blacks that likely biased our results in the previous chapters.

As we learned in chapter 1, many criticisms have been leveled against research that tests the spatial mismatch hypothesis using the central city/suburban dichotomy as the methodological approach. Many have suggested that this methodological approach is limited because it assumes that suburban employment growth uniformly improves—or fails to improve—the economic opportunities of all suburban households. That is, some suburban households may benefit more from a suburban residential location than other suburbanites because they live closer to the nexus of suburban jobs. For example, Ihlanfeldt (1992) argues that in Atlanta, employment growth in the Northern rather than the Southern suburbs has been far superior. However, Atlanta's black suburban population is concentrated in the Southern suburbs, located on the fringe of the central city ghetto. This pattern is not entirely replicated in Prince George's. Although black suburbanization in Prince George's County has occurred in the inner portion of the county that closely borders the Washington, DC city limits, most of Prince George's jobs and job growth has also occurred in this area. Given these dynamics, the Washington, DC metropolitan area is a natural experiment to test the spatial mismatch hypothesis using the comparisons of central city and suburban residents as the methodological approach. The findings from this study will shed light on the validity of the findings from the previous chapters since it was impossible to control for the peculiarities of black and Latino suburbanization in each of the suburbs included in the analysis.

In this chapter, I am interested in the following questions: 1) does suburban residential location improve labor market outcomes as the spatial mismatch hypothesis predicts? 2) are blacks' and Latinos' labor market outcomes better relative to whites in the suburbs than the central city? 3) what is the relative importance of race and space, and their possible interactions, in determining blacks' and Latinos' worse labor market outcomes in relation to whites in metropolitan areas? and 4) does greater discrimination in suburban than central city labor markets reduce the potential employment gains to be made by blacks as a result of having a suburban residential location?

I begin by briefly reviewing the issues related to black suburbanization, particularly as it relates to a study of the spatial mismatch hypothesis. I then describe the "setting" in which this black and Latino suburbanization has taken place. Finally, I present the findings of the research, concluding with a discussion of them.

THE DYNAMICS OF BLACK SUBURBANIZATION

During the past 20 years, blacks' rates of suburbanization has been greater than in previous decades (Stahura 1986; Clay 1979). Blacks' presence in the suburbs increased from 4.8 percent in 1970 to 7.1 percent in 1980 to 8.5 percent in 1990, reversing a trend in which black suburbanization remained stagnant at approximately 4 percent from 1950 to 1960 (Stahura 1986; Schneider and Phelan 1993). In fact, the suburban black population increased faster than the central city black population over the 1970 decade (Long and DeAre 1981). Moreover, this black suburbanization varied regionally.[20] As we have discussed in the previous chapters, the spatial mismatch hypothesis implies that black suburbanization should improve blacks' labor market outcomes. This improvement should result as a consequence of not only blacks proximity to jobs (Kain 1969), but also their proximity to jobs for which they qualify (Kasarda 1985).

However, there are also reasons why blacks who suburbanize may not have better economic opportunities or more favorable labor market outcomes than their central city counterparts. Galster (1991) showed that although blacks did gain access to suburbs in the 1970s, they moved to those parts of the suburbs adjacent to the central cites where jobs have left, while whites moved farther out in the suburbs close to the urban fringe. As a result, Galster argued that "the average black household, though now residing farther from the CBD than before, remains as close to it as ever relative to the average white household" (Galster 1991: 625). Stahura (1988) also found that this pattern of black suburbanization was the dominant form in the 1970s, as did Kain (1985) for the 1980s. In addition, Massey and Denton (1988) argued that blacks remain more segregated in suburbs, though not as highly segregated as their central city counterparts, than any either Asians or Latinos. Blacks move into the aging inner suburbs that concurrently are abandoned or are being abandoned by whites. As Galster argues, "suburban residence per se is not equivalent to desegregation or relief from the burdens of ghetto residence" (Galster 1991: 622).

Not surprisingly, then, this pattern is also supported by other studies that examine suburban blacks in relation to the characteristics of the suburbs. These studies show that suburban blacks tend to live in highly segregated suburbs which are not only close to the central city, but that also possess few jobs (Galster, 1987). Therefore, suburbanization in and of itself, as Kain (1968) and Kasarda (1985) suggest, may not improve black and Latino labor market outcomes relative to their central city counterparts or to their white suburban counterparts. In fact, as Ihlanfeldt (1992) argues, it is researchers' inability to take into consideration where blacks move to in the suburbs that makes economic welfare comparisons of central city and suburban blacks a crude test of the spatial mismatch hypothesis. In order for blacks' and Latinos' labor market outcomes to improve relative to their central city counterparts and relative to their white suburban counterparts, the kinds of suburbs and the location within the suburbs that blacks and Latinos move into must also have better employment opportunities relative to those in the central city. It is crucial, then, that one take into account the kinds of suburbs that blacks move into when using a central city/suburban comparison to test of the spatial mismatch hypothesis.

THE WASHINGTON, DC SETTING

The Washington, DC area represents a natural experiment to test the spatial mismatch hypothesis of black and Latino labor market disadvantage because of the tremendous demographic changes that have occurred in the area over the past two decades (See Figure A5.1 in the appendix for geographic feel). The demography of Prince George's County, MD, a suburb of Washington, DC, has changed dramatically over a twenty year period. Table 5.1 shows Prince George's population changes from 1970 to 1990. In 1970, whites represented the majority of the county population of 660,567. By 1990, however, blacks became the majority of the population, largely due to blacks' in-migration from neighboring Washington, DC (Dent 1992). In addition, between 1980 and 1990 the Latino population increased by nearly 100.0 percent, while others grew by 113.0 percent, adding to the total county population increase of some 70,000 since 1970.

Much of the black population in-migration to Prince George's came from neighboring Washington, DC (Dent 1992) and much of the Latino in-migrants, though not mostly from Washington, DC (Dunn 1991), included the middle-class. However, as Galster (1991) and Massey (1993) have found in their research of blacks who move to the suburbs, blacks and Latinos who in-migrated to Prince George's during the late 1970s and early 1980s moved to that part of the county that most closely neighbored Washington, DC. This part of Prince George's is termed the 'inner beltway'. In fact, in 1990, 66.3 percent of blacks and only 35.6 percent of whites who live in Prince George's took residence inside the 'inner beltway'.[21] Even though in 1990 a majority of blacks lived in the 'inner beltway' of Prince George's, they have, since the early 1980s, increasingly penetrated most other areas of the county that are more distant from Washington, DC (Dent 1992). This 'outer beltway' portion of the county is much more residential, wealthy, and rural than the 'inner beltway' portion.[22] However, unlike the black suburbanization patterns that Galster (1991) and Massey (1993) found, the 'inner beltway' area of Prince George's where the majority of blacks and Latinos in the county live also contains most of the county's

Table 5.1: Prince George's County, MD and Washington, DC Population by Race from 1970 to 1990

	1970		1980		1990	
	Total	Percent	Total	Percent	Total	Percent
Prince George's County						
White	561,482	85.0	393,722	59.2	314,616	43.1
Black	91,819	13.9	247,860	37.2	369,791	50.7
Latino	–		14,421	2.2	29,900	4.1
Other	–		19,287	2.9	45,214	6.2
Total	660,567		665,071		729,268	
Washington, DC						
White	210,878	27.9	174,903	27.4	179,667	30.7
Black	537,570	71.1	448,365	70.2	399,604	68.3
Latino	15,887	2.1	17,873	2.8	32,710	5.6
Other	8,062	1.1	15,065	2.4	5,950	1.0
Total	756,510		638,333		585,221	

Note: Column percent do not add up to 100 because Latinos can be of either white or black racial heritage. Source: 1970, 1980, 1990 *US Census of the Population.*

Table 5.2: Change in Jobs, Employees, and Job Import Ratios in Washington, DC and Prince George's County, MD from 1970 to 1990

	Total Jobs[a]		Total Employees[b]		Job Import Ratio	
	DC	Prince George's	DC	Prince George's	DC	Prince George's
1970	326,584	96,669	244,293	204,029	1.34	.47
% Δ70–80	5.0	66.1	-9.2	28.0	15.7	29.7
1980	342,906	160,609	221,786	261,207	1.55	.61
% Δ80–90	24.5	55.9	11.0	28.6	11.6	23.0
1990	426,959	250,372	246,241	335,992	1.73	.75
% Δ70–90	30.7	159.0	0.8	64.7	29.1	59.6

Source: [a] 1970, 1980, and 1990 *US Census County Business Patterns*. [b] 1970, 1980, and 1990 *US Census of Population*.

commercial activity and economic development, i.e., jobs, and has experienced most of the county's job growth.[23]

An initial inspection of the demand-side of the Washington, DC's, and Prince George's labor markets indicates that job growth has occurred more rapidly in Prince George's than in Washington, DC. Table 5.2 shows the total jobs, total employees, and job import ratios for the two areas between 1970 and 1990.[24] In 1990, it is clear that Prince George's, like other suburban areas in the country, has had much more rapid job growth than the central city, or DC, and its job import ratio has increased relative to that of DC's since 1970, even though the job import ratio for DC was nearly 2.5 times higher than that of Prince George's in 1990.[25] Also, about two-thirds of the total jobs between Washington, DC and Prince George's were located in DC.

Blacks and other minorities own a significant share of Prince George's businesses. More than 9,000, of which many are sizeable ventures, of the county's 25,000 businesses were minority owned in 1987. In fact, it is one of the largest concentrations of minority-owned businesses in the nation (Dunn 1991). Moreover, Bates (1992) finds that minority businesses are more likely to hire minority workers. There is strong reason to believe, then, that residence in Prince George's should in fact improve young black and Latino's labor market outcomes relative to their central city counterparts, and may even improve their labor market status relative to whites in the metropolitan area.

THE ANALYSIS

Data

To examine the importance of space in labor market outcomes across the Prince George's and Washington, DC area, I use data from the 1990 Public Use Micro-Data A(5%)-Sample (PUMA) for the Washington, DC proper, and Prince George's County, MD areas. These data provide individual observations on all of the population and housing variables collected by the *US Census* bureau in 1990. From this dataset, I selected non-Latino white, non-Latino black, and Latino males aged 16–21 who lived at home at the time of the survey. The use of a dataset composed of young people who live at home minimizes the endogeneity problem of residential location and employment status or job location from which many spatial mismatch studies have suffered (Ihlanfeldt, 1992). In addition, it controls for the selectivity of those who are most able to move to the suburbs. I also restricted the dataset to youth with a high school degree or less of education because recent labor market research suggests that these workers are more likely to experience labor market difficulties (Bound and Freeman 1992; Holzer 1993; Bluestone et al. 1994) and are more likely to be adversely affected by the spatial mismatch of job and residential location (Ihlanfeldt 1992).

Suburban/Central City Employment Comparisons

Table 5.3 shows the labor market outcomes of young white, black, and Latino males aged 16 to 21 and the central city concentration of these population groups in the DC and Prince George's County area (hereafter referred to as the PGDC area) for 1990.[26] Young white males have better labor market outcomes than their black and Latino counterparts in the PGDC area. In fact, the spatial mismatch hypothesis predicts that this should be true particularly since a greater percentage of whites live in Prince George's, where job growth has been more rapid than in DC. Moreover, the hypothesis also predicts that suburban residents should perform better, in absolute terms, in the labor market than their central city counterparts. We should expect, then, Prince George's residents' labor market outcomes to be better than their central city counterparts.

Table 5.3: Labor Market Outcomes[a] for Males Aged 16–21 and Washington, DC Concentration[b] of Racial Groups across the Washington, DC and Prince George's County, MD Area: 1990

	White	Black	Latino
Emp Rate	60.3	43.9	50.1
Unemp Rate	10.5	26.3	18.9
Jobless Weeks	34.1	41.4	37.8
Percent of Population living within Washington, DC	36.3	51.9	52.2

Source: [a]Based on author's calculations using the 1990 Public Use Microdata Samples (PUMS). [b]1990 *US Census of the Population.*

Table 5.4 shows the labor market comparisons of young males in DC and Prince George's. Panel A shows the employment and unemployment rates, and jobless weeks for all young white, black and

Table 5.4: Comparisons of Young Men's (Aged 16 to 21) Labor Market Outcomes in Washington, DC and Prince George's County, MD by Race, School Enrollment Status and Education: 1990

	White		Black		Latino	
	DC	Prince George's	DC	Prince George's	DC	Prince George's
A. All						
Emp. Rate	49.7	67.8	39.6	48.1	48.4	54.4
Unemp. Rate	13.5	9.3	28.3	24.0	20.3	17.6
Jobless Weeks	36.1	33.2	42.2	40.5	40.3	35.5
B. Sch. Status						
In School						
Emp. Rate	38.9	52.2	24.3	30.6	32.8	28.1
Unemp. Rate	17.1	12.0	23.4	25.6	10.5	28.9
Jobless Weeks	40.0	35.3	44.6	43.1	41.1	39.8
Out-of-school						
Emp. Rate	65.8	86.7	41.7	50.9	59.2	76.9
Unemp. Rate	11.9	8.8	31.1	20.2	20.5	16.0
Jobless Weeks	37.3	24.7	39.0	36.4	39.4	28.8

Table 5.4: continued

	White		Black		Latino	
	DC	Prince George's	DC	Prince George's	DC	Prince George's
C. Out-of-Sch						
No H.S. Deg.						
Emp. Rate	60.6	78.7	36.6	48.9	57.4	76.4
Unemp. Rate	13.2	9.8	39.8	28.6	23.8	19.1
Jobless Weeks	33.6	27.7	41.8	39.0	40.5	30.2
H.S. Degree						
Emp. Rate	76.3	89.7	61.0	65.8	64.7	71.6
Unemp. Rate	10.5	7.3	18.2	16.2	11.5	11.7
Jobless Weeks	26.8	22.3	31.5	31.8	37.0	26.2

Source: Based on author's calculations using the 1990 Public Use Micro-data Samples (PUMS).

Latino males in 1990.[27] In general, white, black, and Latino males do seem to perform better by these labor market indicators in Prince George's than in DC. Prince George's male residents have higher employment rates, lower unemployment rates, and fewer jobless weeks than their DC counterparts. For example, white, black, and Latino males' unemployment rates in Prince George's are 45, 18, and 15 percent lower, respectively, than those of their DC counterparts.

The results from Panel A include both those in- and out-of-school. Their interpretation, then, can be misleading since schooling, in many instances, competes with market work. Panel B shows these same labor market outcomes for those who are in- and out-of-school. The differences in employment rates between those who are in- and out-of-school for all young males confirms that those who are in-school tend not to enter the labor market at the same rate as those out-of-school. Isolating those who are out-of-school and more attached to the labor market than those in-school shows that, again, residence in Prince George's appears to improve young males' labor market performance relative to their central city counterparts. Moreover, judging from the higher employment rates for these groups in PG than in DC, out-of-school Prince George's residents may also participate more in the labor force than their DC counterparts. This is particularly true for Prince George's young white and Latino males, whose employment rate is 21.1 and 23.0 percentage points higher, respectively, than that of their DC counterparts.

Those who are out-of-school could have either received their high school degree or dropped out of high school without it. Certainly, those who are out-of-school and possess a high school diploma should perform better in the labor market than those who do not because of the additional skills that they bring to the market or because they are more likely to pass employers' screening tests. Panel C compares the labor market outcomes of young out-of-school males in Prince George's and DC by whether or not they received a high school degree. First, as expected, for out-of-school male youth, those without a high school degree perform more poorly in the labor market than those with a high school degree in both Prince George's and DC, although there are fewer differences for whites, and to some extent Latinos, than for blacks. This suggests that for young black males in the PGDC area, attainment of a high school degree may be just as important in improving their labor market standing as having a residential location in Prince George's. Second, for those who are out-of-school, both those with and without a high school degree have better labor market outcomes if they live in Prince George's as opposed to DC. However, the improvements are much more pronounced for whites, and to some extent Latinos, than they are for blacks with respect to the employment rate and jobless weeks.

Taken together, these labor market indicators suggest that, in general, young males in Prince George's do have better labor market outcomes than their DC counterparts. These findings are not in contradiction with the spatial mismatch hypothesis and may go a long way in explaining racial labor market outcome differences in the PGDC area. Given the logic of the spatial mismatch hypothesis, racial differences in labor market outcomes should not be larger in Prince George's than in DC. In other words, the spatial mismatch suggests that because of the better job opportunities in the suburbs, blacks' and Latinos' labor market status should improve as much as their white counterparts given a suburban residential location. After all, the spatial mismatch hypothesis attempts to explain not only the absolute labor market differences between blacks and Latinos in the cities and suburbs, but the racial differences in labor market outcomes within metropolitan areas as well. If the racial labor market outcome differences are larger in Prince George's than in DC, it is difficult to say that a spatial mismatch between jobs and residential location alone is the major explanation of racial labor market differences in the PGDC area.

Table 5.7 shows the black/white and Latino/white labor market outcome ratios for young males living in Washington, DC and Prince George's in 1990. In general, young black and Latino males' relative labor market status is worse in Prince George's than in DC. This is particularly true for out-of-school young black males with a high school degree whose employment rate and unemployment rate climbs from being 20 percent lower and 73 percent higher, respectively, than those of their white counterparts in DC, to being 27 lower and 122 percent higher, respectively, than those of their white counterparts in Prince George's. These results support the findings from chapter 3 which also suggest that young white males benefit more than either young black or Latino males from a suburban residential location.

Table 5.5: Comparisons of Black/White and Latino/White Labor Market Outcome Ratios for Males Aged 16–21 in Washington, DC and Prince George's County, MD by School Enrollment Status and Education: 1990

	Black/White Ratio		Latino/White Ratio	
	DC	Prince George's	DC	Prince George's
A. All				
Emp. Rate	.80	.71	.97	.80
Unemp. Rate	2.10	2.58	1.50	1.89
Jobless Weeks	1.17	1.22	1.12	1.07
B. School Status				
Out-of-school				
Emp. Rate	.63	.58	.90	.89
Unemp. Rate	2.61	2.30	1.72	1.81
Jobless Weeks	1.05	1.47	1.06	1.17
C. Out-of-School				
No H.S. Degree				
Emp. Rate	.60	.62	.94	.97
Unemp. Rate	3.02	2.92	1.80	1.95
Jobless Weeks	1.24	1.41	1.21	1.09
H.S. Degree				
Emp. Rate	.80	.73	.85	.80
Unemp. Rate	1.73	2.22	1.10	1.60
Jobless Weeks	1.18	1.43	1.38	1.17

Nonetheless, there are some cases where the racial labor market outcome ratios as measured by one of the labor market performance indicators does improve in Prince George's as compared to DC, but these improvements are slight and not as dramatic as the relative losses. These relative improvements of black and Latinos are mainly found for out-of-school youth without a high school degree. These results support Kasarda's (1985) hypothesis that suburban labor markets may have better employment opportunities for less-skilled blacks than those in the central city because the decentralization of jobs has mainly occurred for those that are low-skill. Nonetheless, blacks' labor market position in relation to whites is worse than Latinos' relative position in both areas, though the racial differences are striking in both locations. Although these results do not prove prima facie that employment discrimination exists, or that if it does exist that it may be much stronger in Prince George's than in DC's labor market, they also do nothing to refute such claims. But these results are also consistent with the possibility that a larger concentration of whites with more human capital stock than blacks or Latinos live in PG, since better educated, as opposed to less educated, youth are more likely to do well in the labor market, irrespective of their residential location

As predicted by the spatial mismatch hypothesis, this section shows that, in general, young males possess better labor market outcomes when they live in Prince George's rather than in DC. However, the racial differences in these labor market outcomes are more stark in Prince George's than in DC. These results cast serious doubt on the ability of the spatial mismatch hypothesis alone to explain the racial labor market outcome differences across the PGDC area, since greater employment discrimination and greater human capital accumulation by whites can also explain these differences. The next section attempts to examine the relative importance of "space" and "race" in explaining the racial differences in labor market outcomes across the PGDC area.

The Effect of Suburban Residential Location on Employment

I use regression techniques to investigate whether and to what extent a Prince George's suburban residential location increases the probability of young white, black and Latino males' employment, controlling for relevant personal and family background variables. I examine this question by running pooled regressions over the Prince George's and DC area for each racial group. The basic estimating equation can be expressed as:

$$\Pr(E) = f(\text{Residential Location, Personal and Family Background Characteristics}) \tag{5.1}$$

where P(E) is the probability of employment.

The 1990 PUMS provides a number of personal and family background variables that may affect the probability of youth employment. Personal characteristics that may affect the probability of having a job include the youth's age, whether or not the youth is enrolled-in-school, and if out-of-school, whether or not the youth graduated from high school, and whether or not the youth has a child.[28] Family background characteristics that may affect the probability of having a job include whether the youth lives in a one-parent, female-headed household, and family income.[29] These variables are defined in Table 5.6.

Descriptive Statistics

Table 5.7 shows the personal and family background means and standard deviations for employed and jobless young males in Prince George's and DC. Employed youth are, on average, older, less likely to be enrolled-in-school, more likely to hold a high school degree than are the jobless in both areas for each racial group. The employed also have higher family incomes than the jobless. One exception is jobless young white males in DC, whose family income is, on average, higher than that of their employed counterparts. Since their school enrollment mean (.64) is higher than that of their employed counterparts, many of these jobless youth probably engage in other nonwork activities that tend to pull them out of the labor force. The employed are, on average, less likely to come from a female headed household, except for young white males in DC, and are less likely to have a child, except for Latino's in Prince George's.

A comparison of each racial group in DC and Prince George's shows that employed or jobless young white males are more likely to be enrolled-in-school, more likely to have a high school degree, and more likely to have higher family incomes than either employed or jobless young black or Latino males. These differences are likely to contribute to the racial differences in labor market outcomes that we saw in Table 5.5.

The means and standard deviations of the variables in the models are provided in Table 5.8. Young white males across DC and Prince George's are more likely to be enrolled-in-school, to have a high school degree, are more likely to have family income in the highest income category, and are more likely to live in Prince George's than their black or Latino counterparts. However, they are less likely than their black or Latino counterparts to live in the 'inner beltway' portion of Prince George's. Young white males are less likely to have a child and less

Table 5.6: Definition of Variables

Personal Characteristics
Age of youth in years
Enrolled-in-school (1=enrolled)
Youth high school dropout (1=dropout)
Youth has high school degree (1=graduate)
Youth has child (1=child)

Family Background
Youth lives in one-parent—female-headed household (1=yes)
Youth lives in two-parent—at least two adults (1=yes)
Family Income (reference category) $25,000 and < $75,000
Family Income > $0 and <$25,000 (1=yes)
Family Income > $75,000 (1=yes)

Residential Location
Residence in District of Columbia (1=yes)
Residence in Prince George's (1=yes)
Residence in Inner Beltway of Prince George's (1=yes)
Residence in Outer Beltway of Prince George's (1=yes)

likely to come from a female headed household than their black or Latino counterparts. Thus, in addition to young white males being more concentrated in Prince George's, where job access is superior to that of DC, a key factor that can also contribute to creating the racial employment gap in the DC metropolitan area is education. Even though young white males have higher family incomes, its effect on their employment rate and in closing or widening the racial employment gap in the metropolitan area is ambiguous. Families with high income create better job opportunities for other family members (Cain and Finnie 1990). However, since the dataset includes those in-school, families with high income may influence or require that their children participate in nonwork activities such as after-school sports, which would have the effect of decreasing their participation in the labor force and lowering their employment rate.

Model Results

The model results are shown in Table 5.9.[30] Model 1 shows the effect of a Prince George's (PG) residential location on employment, while Model 2 shows the effect of location within PG, i.e., 'inner' (PGIB) vs. 'outer' (PGOB) beltway, on employment. In these models, I interacted

Table 5.7: Personal and Family Background Means for Employed and Jobless by Race and Residential Location: 1990

	Age	Sch. Enroll.	H.S. Dropout	H.S. Degree	Family Inc. (median)	Female Head	Child
White							
DC							
Employed	18.6 (1.5)	.64 (.35)	.10 (.22)	.25 (.43)	$45,121 (60,251)	.09 (.28)	.10 (.13)
Jobless	18.2 (1.4)	.75 (.23)	.11 (.24)	.14 (.31)	$55,723 (69,211)	.03 (.16)	.11 (.13)
Prin. Geor.							
Employed	18.8 (1.7)	.59 (.50)	.19 (.39)	.24 (.50)	$46,000 (40,773)	.05 (.22)	.09 (.14)
Jobless	17.4 (1.3)	.69 (.38)	.11 (.31)	.18 (.37)	$41,975 (43,657)	.09 (.28)	.11 (.16)
Black							
DC							
Employed	19.2 (1.6)	.52 (.45)	.30 (.47)	.18 (.36)	$33,606 (28,008)	.08 (.28)	.12 (.16)
Jobless	18.0 (1.6)	.55 (.49)	.30 (.47)	.16 (.32)	$21,248 (30,655)	.15 (.31)	.16 (.15)
Prin. Geor.							
Employed	18.9 (1.6)	.54 (.49)	.19 (.36)	.27 (.43)	$50,400 (30,866)	.09 (.29)	.11 (.14)
Jobless	17.5 (1.4)	.66 (.41)	.13 (.30)	.21 (.43)	$44,610 (28,381)	.15 (.36)	.14 (.16)

Table 5.7 continued

	Age	Sch. Enroll.	H.S. Dropout	H.S. Degree	Family Inc. (median)	Female Head	Child
			Latino				
DC							
Employed	19.0	.33	.48	.19	$26,000	.06	.14
	(1.4)	(.46)	(.50)	(.34)	(28,326)	(.23)	(.18)
Jobless	18.7	.55	.31	.14	$12,000	.08	.16
	(1.7)	(.50)	(.47)	(.30)	(32,738)	(.27)	(.21)
Prin. Geor.							
Employed	19.1	.35	.40	.25	$37,166	.05	.17
	(1.6)	(.46)	(.49)	(.49)	(34,227)	(.21)	(.20)
Jobless	17.5	.65	.17	.18	$45,860	.09	.13
	(1.4)	(.41)	(.33)	(.39)	(30,519)	(.29)	(.16)

Table 5.8: Means (Standard Deviations) for Residential Location Equations

Variable	White			Black			Latino		
	Total	PG	DC	Total	PG	DC	Total	PG	DC
Employed	.60	.68	.50	.44	.49	.40	.50	.54	.48
	(.50)	(.48)	(.46)	(.49)	(.50)	(.48)	(.50)	(.50)	(.50)
Age	18.2	18.3	18.1	18.3	18.2	18.4	18.6	18.3	19.0
	(1.7)	(1.7)	(1.4)	(1.7)	(1.7)	(1.7)	(1.7)	(1.7)	(1.6)
Enrlld. Sch.	.67	.63	.75	.58	.62	.54	.50	.56	.44
	(.47)	(.49)	(.29)	(.49)	(.49)	(.50)	(.50)	(.50)	(.50)
H.S. Dropout	.14	.14	.13	.22	.14	.30	.32	.25	.40
	(.35)	(.37)	(.22)	(.41)	(.34)	(.46)	(.47)	(.49)	(.49)
H.S. Degree	.18	.23	.12	.20	.24	.16	.18	.19	.17
	(.39)	(.37)	(.22)	(.40)	(.43)	(.37)	(.38)	(.40)	(.37)
Child	.10	.09	.11	.12	.11	.14	.15	.15	.15
	(.13)	(.14)	(.11)	(.15)	(.15)	(.16)	(.17)	(.17)	(.16)
Female Head	.06	.07	.05	.15	.13	.18	.07	.07	.06
(FHH)	(.24)	(.25)	(.22)	(.36)	(.33)	(.39)	(.25)	(.25)	(.25)
Two Parent	.94	.93	.95	.85	.87	.82	.93	.93	.94
(TPH)	(.50)	(.50)	(.50)	(.49)	(.50)	(.43)	(.50)	(.50)	(.49)

Table 5.8 continued

	White			Black			Latino		
Variable	Total	PG	DC	Total	PG	DC	Total	PG	DC
Family Income ($0–<$25,000)	.26 (.39)	.18 (.35)	.54 (.50)	.34 (.40)	.21 (.39)	.45 (.43)	.32 (.43)	.18 (.40)	.47 (.44)
Family Income ($25,000–$75,000)	.45 (.50)	.54 (.50)	.14 (.34)	.54 (.50)	.60 (.49)	.49 (.50)	.52 (.50)	.60 (.49)	.43 (.50)
Family Income (>$75,000)	.29 (.45)	.28 (.45)	.32 (.47)	.12 (.33)	.19 (.39)	.06 (.24)	.16 (.37)	.22 (.41)	.10 (.30)
Dist. of Columbia (DC)	.20 (.40)	—	—	.52 (.50)	—	—	.47 (.50)	—	—
Prince George's (PG)	.80 (.40)	—	—	.48 (.50)	—	—	.53 (.50)	—	—
Inner Beltway (PGIB)	.30 (.46)	.37 (.48)	—	.35 (.48)	.72 (.45)	—	.38 (.49)	.72 (.45)	—
Outer Beltway (PGOB)	.50 (.50)	.63 (.48)	—	.14 (.34)	.28 (.45)	—	.15 (.36)	.28 (.45)	—

Table 5.9: Pooled Employment Equations Across Residential Location for Young White, Black, and Latino Males (standard errors in parentheses)

Variable	White Model 1	White Model 2	Black Model 1	Black Model 2	Latino Model 1	Latino Model 2
Constant	-.975** (.356)	-1.023** (.359)	-1.302*** (.218)	-1.293*** (.204)	-.703 (.466)	-.605 (.468)
Age	.076*** (.021)	.079*** (.021)	.095*** (.012)	.094*** (.012)	.059** (.027)	.053** (.027)
Child	-.069 (.071)	-.063 (.071)	-.070 (.051)	-.071 (.051)	-.011 (.107)	.005 (.108)
FHH x Fam. Inc. ($0–<$25,000)	-.397*** (.163)	-.401*** (.163)	-.090* (.052)	-.091* (.052)	.101 (.248)	.095 (.248)
TPH x Fam. Inc. ($0–<$25,000)	-.130** (.060)	-.123** (.061)	-.180*** (.032)	-.178*** (.032)	-.073 (.076)	-.077 (.077)
Family Income (>$75,000)	-.020 (.049)	-.026 (.050)	-.039 (.040)	-.033 (.040)	-.034 (.090)	-.069 (.093)
H.S. Dropout x DC	.077 (.206)	.071 (.206)	.004 (.043)	.005 (.043)	.236** (.101)	.235** (.101)
H.S. Degree x DC	.225 (.229)	.214 (.230)	.196*** (.055)	.198*** (.055)	.238* (.136)	.241* (.135)
Enrlld. Sch. x PG	.227*** (.060)	—	.044 (.034)	—	.027 (.098)	—
H.S. Dropout x PG	.308*** (.078)	—	.127** (.057)	—	.332*** (.113)	—

Table 5.9 continued

Variable	White Model 1	White Model 2	Black Model 1	Black Model 2	Latino Model 1	Latino Model 2
H.S. Degree x PG	.482*** (.080)	—	.323*** (.050)	—	.317*** (.125)	—
Enrlld. Sch. x PGIB	—	.168** (.071)	—	.053 (.046)	—	-.005 (.105)
H.S. Dropout x PGIB	—	.342*** (.098)	—	.171*** (.063)	—	.344*** (.116)
H.S. Degree x PGIB	—	.478*** (.104)	—	.352*** (.053)	—	.189 (.144)
Enrlld. Sch. x PGOB	—	.268*** (.065)	—	.023 (.049)	—	.090 (.138)
H.S. Dropout x PGOB	—	.272** (.097)	—	-.021 (.107)	—	.165 (.342)
H.S. Degree x PGOB	—	.478*** (.089)	—	.232*** (.087)	—	.567*** (.186)
Adj. R^2	.210	.214	.207	.210	.153	.168
Standard Error	.446	.446	.438	.438	.472	.471
N	725	725	1,360	1,360	394	394

the educational variables with the residential location variables because I assumed that the effect of education on employment varied in the different residential areas. That is, I assumed that employers in the PGDC area may value a high school degree from, or a student who attends a PG school, more than a degree from or a student who goes to a DC school. Also, even within PG, employers may value an education more from an 'outer beltway' rather than an 'inner beltway' school because the 'outer beltway' houses wealthier residents, which usually implies better schools. Of course, in order to make this assumption, I also assumed that youth went to schools in the areas that they live since the *US Census* provides no data on the location of the individual's school. Because few youth in the sample have moved from 1985 to 1990 to PG or DC, this is likely a fair assumption.[31] I also assumed that youth are more likely to work in their residential area. For comparison, I ran these models without the interactions, assuming that the education variables' slopes were the same in each residential area. The results of these models are in the appendix, Table A5.2. These results have a slightly different interpretation and I will refer to them in this section where appropriate.

The results from Model 1 show that, in general, a residential location in PG is a significant factor in young white and black, but not Latino, males' likelihood of having a job for every education category, controlling for relevant personal and family background characteristics, in the PGDC area. The exceptions are enrolled-in-school in PG for both young black and Latino males, as this variable is not significant for these groups. Given that the reference variable for these interacted variables is enrolled-in-school and living in DC, the significance of the enrolled-in-school in PG variable for whites is interesting, particularly since enrolled-in-school young white males in DC have a higher employment rate than either their black or Latino counterparts (see Table 5.4). Since these variables are significant for whites and because more of white males live in PG than either their black or Latino counterparts, it appears as though white males' greater residential concentration in PG may explain part of the racial employment rate differences across the PGDC area as the spatial mismatch hypothesis suggests. Nonetheless, it is clear that a residential location in PG matters greatly for young white males, and matters somewhat for young black and Latino males in obtaining employment, controlling for educational levels and other relevant variables.

Although the interacted education-residential location variables are, in general, significant and positive in the employment rate equations for young males, their effect on having a job, in general, is much stronger for young white than it is for either young black or Latino males. The one exception is young Latino male high school dropouts in PG whose employment advantage over their enrolled-in-school in DC counterparts is slightly greater than that of whites. This suggests that young black, and to a certain extent Latino, males may not be treated the same way as whites in PG's labor markets and may explain why their relative labor market status to whites is worse in PG than in DC.

Note that the significant education-residential location interacted variables for PG are stronger in magnitude than the ones in DC for young black and Latino males, while the ones for young whites in DC are not significant. For black and Latino males, this suggests that both the lack of jobs in DC and the value of a PG education to employers may explain their greater likelihood of having a job in PG than in DC. Young, out-of-school white males in DC are no more likely to hold a job than their enrolled-in-school counterparts. This suggests that young white males in DC of any education level have little difficulty in getting jobs since their employment rates are much higher than those of blacks and Latinos in DC. Out-of -school, young black males in DC do not have an employment advantage over their enrolled-in-school counterparts. Table 5.4 shows that their employment rate is lower than that of any other out-of-school group in either residential area. These results suggest that either inner-city young black males are the hardest to employ, or as Neckerman and Kirschenman (1991) note, they may be the least preferred workers to employers. That is, if DC employers engage in statistical discrimination in hiring, they may weigh receipt of a high school degree more heavily for young black males, whom they might view as having "uncertain productivities," than for young white males, whom they might view as having more "certain productivities." Young black males, then, are "penalized" in the labor market by employers more than comparable young white males if they do not possess a high school degree.[32]

Note that high school dropouts have an employment advantage over their enrolled-in-school counterparts, which is likely the result of more enrolled-in-school members being out-of-the-labor-force than their high school drop out counterparts. Also note that high school degree holders have an employment advantage over their counterparts without degrees, as one should expect.

Other significant factors that are associated with an employment advantage include age. Young white, black, and Latino males' employment advantage increase as these youth get older. It is likely that since many younger teenagers are enrolled-in-school they are less likely to be in the labor force and work than their older out-of-school counterparts. Since school enrollment is controlled for in these models this is an unlikely explanation for its significance on employment. The significance of age on employment also suggests that older or more mature youth may be more likely to hold or get a job. The age difference of youth in the dataset is only five years, and this difference may not be large enough for sharp maturation differences to be noticed. A more likely scenario is that the significance of age on employment is generated by employers avoidance of hiring younger teenagers and, conversely, their preference of hiring older youth, because they may view they former as unreliable and unstable.

Family income levels also affect youth's ability to get jobs. Accordingly, I split the family income measure into three variables representing low, moderate, and high family income levels.[33] In addition, I interacted the low family income variable with female headed household and two parent household status to compare the effect of these household types on youth employment. Youth in female headed households generally suffer from a one earner, low-income household and not necessarily from family dysfunction. Low income households may have a negative effect on youth employment because they may have fewer job contacts than families with more income. On the other hand, youth in female headed households may feel more compelled to work to help in the household than youth in other family structures with low income.

The results in Table 5.9 show that family income does not have a significant effect on young Latino males' employment, and that high family income does not have a significant effect on all groups' employment. Both the interacted low family income variables have a significant, negative effect on employment for young white and black males. These results imply that the effect of low income in limiting job opportunities for young people as a result of fewer job contacts applies equally to female headed or two parent households. However, the negative effect of low income female headed households on young white males' employment is stronger than that of their young black male counterparts, while the negative effect of low income two parent households on employment is stronger for young black than for young white males. These results suggest that the limited job contact role of low family income in female headed households is much stronger in the case of young white males than the increased work effort role of these youth in female headed households on employment. While this is also true for young black males, the smaller negative coefficient on this variable implies that the increased work effort to help in the household is much stronger for young black than it is for young white males. The greater magnitude of blacks' negative two parent household low income coefficient in relation to that of whites suggests that the limited job contact role in reducing youth's employment opportunities is more prevalent for blacks.

Model 2 includes location identifiers for the 'inner beltway' and 'outer beltway' part of Prince George's.[34] Since all of the other control variables remain virtually the same as those in Model 1, I will concentrate on the interacted residence-education variables. A majority of PG's jobs are located and job growth has occurred in the 'inner beltway' portion of the county. It is reasonable to expect, then, that young white, black, and Latino males should be better off with respect to access to employment living in the 'inner beltway' as opposed to the 'outer beltway' of PG. Model 2 shows that young white males living in the 'inner beltway' portion of PG have an advantage of getting a job compared to their enrolled-in-school DC counterparts in every educational category, while only out-of-school young black males in PGIB have an advantage of getting a job compared to their enrolled-in-school DC counterparts. Only young Latino males who are high school dropouts in PG have an advantage over their enrolled-in-school DC counterparts. For these groups, then, the combination of job concentration and schooling quality in PGIB leads to increased employment opportunities. However, it is clear that the employment opportunities are better for young white males than either young black or Latino males since all of their educational coefficients are significant and their magnitude is greater, or as great, as the other groups' significant variables.

The 'outer beltway' of PG is much more rural and residential than the 'inner beltway.' Given this context, the results of the PGOB interacted variables are interesting. While young white males in PGOB enjoy an employment advantage over their enrolled-in-school DC counterparts, only young black and Latino males in PGOB with high school degrees enjoy an employment advantage over their enrolled-in-school DC counterparts. This suggests that where there are few jobs in the suburbs, employers may be more inclined to hire young white males at any educational level rather than young black or Latino males without high school degrees or who are still in-school. Employers appear to hire young black and Latino males only when they possess a high school degree, or when they have concrete "information" on these workers' productivities. But like the results in DC, the flip-side of this story is that out-of-school, young black, and in this case young Latino, males without a high school degree are penalized more in the PGOB labor market than their white male counterparts. These results suggest that young white males appear to have less difficulty than young black or Latino males in attaining employment irrespective of their residential location or the availability of jobs in that location.

The following analysis of Model 2's results show that a residential location in job-rich suburbs does matter in increasing the employment opportunities of young white, black, and Latino males. However, the analysis also suggests that the opportunities appear greater for whites than for either blacks or Latinos. The spatial mismatch suggests that young white males' higher employment rate than comparable blacks or Latinos in the PGDC area results from their greater concentration in the suburbs where jobs are located. Their higher employment rate could also result from whites' preferential treatment by employers and whites' greater stock of educational attainment in the suburbs. Alternatively, greater racial discrimination in suburban labor markets may limit the potential employment gains that blacks and Latinos can achieve by living in the suburbs. This next section attempts to sort out this relative importance of race and space as determinants of whites' higher employment rate in the PGDC area.[35]

The Contribution of Race and Space to Racial Differences in Employment

One way to test for the relative importance of space and race as contributors to the racial employment differential in the PGDC area is to decompose the racial gap in employment following Oaxaca (1973) and Blinder (1973) decomposition techniques. Given this method, the racial employment gap can be decomposed into differences attributable to the coefficients and differences attributable to the mean values of the variables. The coefficients represent labor market treatment, and the

The Confounding Influence of Race in Space

mean values of the variables represent endowments of the different racial groups. Endowment refers to the stock of individual characteristics that are fixed in one point in time such as the educational level of youth. If we use the case of blacks and whites, for example, the racial employment rate differential ($E^W - E^B$), or .16 as shown in Table 5.8, can be decomposed as follows:

$$(E^W - E^B) = (B_o^W - B_o^B) + \sum_j \bar{X}_j^B (\beta_j^W - \beta_j^B) + \sum_j \beta_j^W (\bar{X}_j^W - \bar{X}_j^B) \quad (5.2)$$

where W and B refer to the white and black samples, respectively, B_o refers to the constant term, X refers to the sample means, and β refers to the *j*th variable's coefficient. The first term on the right hand side of the equation is the portion of the racial gap attributable to differences in the constant terms. This represents differences in treatment (race) that are unexplained by the variables used in the regression. The second term also represents differences in treatment (race), or how differently blacks and whites are treated in the labor market; in this case it tells us how much of the gap is due to the differences in the black and white coefficients. The third term tells how much of the gap is due to differences in the racial means of the variables (or differences in endowments). For example, this term tells us how much of the racial gap in employment is explained by the greater proportion of whites living in the suburbs than that of blacks.

Table 5.10 and Table 5.11 show the results of this decomposition method on the black-white and Latino-white employment rate difference, respectively, in the PGDC area. Table 5.10 shows that the most important sources of the overall black-white gap are age and residential location in PGOB for every education level. Since a larger share of the black sample lives in PGIB than the comparable white sample, we might expect to find blacks making up employment ground in relation to whites. However, the interacted variables for PGIB show that although blacks do have a slight endowment advantage in PGIB in comparison to whites, the treatment of blacks in this area effectively wipes out any of these advantages on employment. The one exception

Table 5.10: Decomposition of Black-White Racial Employment Rate Difference (based on Model 2's results from Table 5.9)

Variable	X^w	X^b	Attributable to Treatment $X^b(B_W - B_B)$	Attributable to Endowments $B^w(X^w - X^b)$	Total
Age	18.2	18.3	-.2745	-.0079	-.2824
Child	.100	.120	.0010	.0013	.0023
FHH x Fam. Inc.	.017	.078	-.0242	.0245	.003
TPH x Fam. Inc.	.237	.257	.0141	.0025	.0166
Family Income	.291	.123	.0009	-.0044	-.0035
H.S. Dropout x DC	.010	.154	.0102	-.0102	0
H.S. Degree x DC	.008	.084	.0013	-.0163	-.0150
Enrlld. Sch. x PGIB	.170	.205	.0236	-.0059	.0177
H.S. Dropout x PGIB	.063	.051	.0087	.0041	.0128
H.S. Degree x PGIB	.063	.093	.0117	-.0143	-.0026
Enrlld. Sch. x PGOB	.321	.097	.0238	.0600	.0838
H.S. Dropout x PGOB	.071	.015	.0044	.0152	.0196
H.S. Degree x PGOB	.111	.025	.0062	.0411	.0473
			-.1928	.0834	
$B_o^W - B_o^B$			.2700		
			.0772		

Note: A negative sign is favorable to blacks.

Table 5.11: Decomposition of Latino-White Ethnic Employment Rate Difference (based on Model 2's results from Table 5.9)

Variable	X^w	X^l	Attributable to Treatment $X^l(B_W - B_L)$	Attributable to Endowments $B^w(X^w - X^l)$	Total
Age	18.2	18.6	.4836	-.0316	.4520
Child	.100	.150	-.0102	.0032	-.0070
FHH x Fam. Inc.	.017	.018	-.0089	.0004	-.0085
TPH x Fam. Inc.	.237	.303	-.0139	.0081	-.0058
Family Income	.291	.162	.0070	-.0034	.0036
H.S. Dropout x DC	.010	.189	-.0310	-.0127	-.0437
H.S. Degree x DC	.008	.079	-.0021	-.0152	-.0173
Enrlld. Sch. x PGIB	.170	.189	.0327	-.0032	.0295
H.S. Dropout x PGIB	.063	.123	-.0002	-.0205	-.0207
H.S. Degree x PGIB	.063	.066	.0191	-.0014	.0177
Enrlld. Sch. x PGOB	.321	.105	.0187	.0580	.0767
H.S. Dropout x PGOB	.071	.009	.0010	.0169	.0179
H.S. Degree x PGOB	.111	.035	-.0031	.0363	.0332
			.4927	.0349	
$B_0^W - B_0^L$			-.4180		
			.0747		

Note: A negative sign is favorable to Latinos.

Table 5.12: Contribution of Prince George's Residential Location to Racial Employment Rate Differential (based on Model's 2 results from Table 5.9)

Method	White-Black Emp. Rate Diff.	% of Emp. Rate Gap Explained	White-Latino Emp. Rate Diff.	% of Emp. Rate Gap Explained
Oaxaca and Blinder	.16		.11	
PG				
Endowment (space)	.06	63	.02	81
Treatment (race)	.08	50	.04	63
PGIB				
Endowment (space)	.18	-13	.14	-27
Treatment (race)	.12	25	.06	64
PGOB				
Endowment (space)	.04	75	0	100
Treatment (race)	.13	19	.09	18
Partial Decomposition				
PG				
Groups own coefficients and White means, Endowment	.10	38	-.03	127
Whites own coefficients and Groups means, Treatment	.02	88	-.04	136
PGIB				
Endowment (space)	.13	19	.08	27
Treatment (race)	.06	63	.01	91
PGOB				
Endowment (space)	.13	19	.01	91
Treatment (race)	.12	25	.06	45

is those with a high school degree in PGIB. However, blacks total advantage in this category is slight and reduces very little of the black-white employment gap.

The results for the PGOB interacted variables are interesting as well. Young white males endowment advantage in PGOB for every educational category explains much more of the racial employment difference, according to this method, than does treatment of blacks. Since there are fewer jobs in this part of the county, white employment gains in this area are generated more by their human capital stock than by their easier job accessibility. However, the combined effect of this endowment advantage of whites and the negative treatment of blacks in this area contribute the most to the racial employment gap.[36] This interpretation must be taken cautiously, though, since the interacted variables Enrlld. Sch. x PGOB and H.S. Dropout x PGOB are not significant in the black equation. Since they are not significant, it is unlikely that any of the racial employment gap would be eliminated if blacks' endowments for these variables were made equal to those of whites.

Both the treatment and endowments of age are favorable to blacks. However, the result of age is difficult to interpret. If employers prefer older workers, especially for blacks, then the gap attributable to treatment for blacks would actually be interpreted as unfavorable treatment towards blacks.

Overall, the results show that slightly more of the racial gap in employment is due to differences in endowment than in treatment. In fact, 48 percent of the white-black employment rate difference can be explained by differential treatment of blacks and whites in the PGDC area, while 52 percent of this difference can be explained by endowment differences by blacks and whites. This suggest that both race and endowments such as education, space, and family structure are equally important factors that explain racial differences in metropolitan areas. According to this method, if blacks kept their same equation structure, but their endowments were made equal to those of whites, their employment would be about 8 percentage points higher in the PGDC area. If they kept the same endowments but faced the white equation structure (treatment), their employment would be 8 percentage points higher as well. As stated earlier, this treatment effect may be understated if employers prefer older rather than younger youth.

Table 5.11 shows that, like the black-white employment differences, the most important sources of the Latino-white employment gap of 11 percentage points are age and the combined effect of residence and education. A slightly larger share of the Latino sample lives in PGIB than comparable whites, and because this area is where the majority of jobs are in PG we should expect to find Latinos make up some employment ground in relation to whites. However, the interacted variables for PGIB show that although Latinos do have a slight endowment advantage, the treatment of Latinos in this area is stronger than the endowment advantage. The one exception is for those without a high school degree in PGIB. These results are similar to the ones for blacks in this area. Again, the interpretation of these decompositions results, particularly for the endowment side, must be taken cautiously since the variables Enrlld. Sch. x PGIB and H.S. Degree x PGIB are not significant in the Latino equation.

Like the case of blacks, much more of the Latino-white employment differential is due to whites' clear endowment advantage in PGOB. Again, these results are interesting because there are fewer jobs and less job growth in this part of the county. Young white males' endowment advantage in PGOB for every educational category explains much more of the racial employment difference, according to this method, than does the treatment of Latinos. Since there are fewer jobs in this part of the county, white employment gains in this area are more likely to be generated by their human capital stock than by their easier job accessibility. Once again, this interpretation must be taken cautiously since the interacted variables Enrlld. Sch. x PGOB and H.S. Dropout x PGOB are not significant in the Latino equation. As in the case of blacks, since they are not significant, it is unlikely that if Latino's endowments for these variables were made equal to those of whites that any of the racial employment gap would be eliminated.[37]

Note that Latino high school dropouts in DC receive both favorable treatment and have an endowment advantage over their white counterparts. These factors, in fact, lower the racial employment gap between these two groups. The greater demand for Latino low-skill workers, particularly Mexican and central American immigrants, in the inner-city is a likely cause of these favorable results for Latinos (Newman 1990).

While the treatment of age is unfavorable to Latinos, they have a slight endowment advantage in age over their white counterparts. Like the case of blacks, this result is difficult to interpret. Again, if employers prefer older workers, then the gap attributable to treatment for Latinos can be actually interpreted as more favorable, rather than

The Confounding Influence of Race in Space 127

unfavorable, treatment towards Latinos, since the magnitude of their age coefficient is smaller than that of whites. If this is true, then the unfavorable treatment of Latinos in relation to whites in the PGDC area will be overstated.

Overall, the results show that more of the racial gap in employment is due to differences in treatment than endowment. In fact, 68 percent of the white-Latino employment rate difference can be explained by differential treatment of Latinos and whites in the PGDC area, while 32 percent of this difference can be explained by endowment differences between Latinos and whites. This suggests that race in the PGDC area is more important than the combined effect of space and other control variables such as education in generating racial employment differences. If Latinos kept the same equation structure, but their endowments were made equal to that of whites, their employment would be about 3 percentage points higher. If they kept the same endowments but faced the white equation structure (treatment), their employment would be 7 percentage points higher. As stated earlier, this treatment effect may be overstated if employers prefer older rather than younger youth.

The following decomposition analysis shows that race and space are important factors in the PGDC area generating racial differences in employment. In addition, race is as important in the case of blacks and more important in the case of Latinos than differences in endowments between these groups and whites in explaining racial employment differences in the PGDC area. However, the following decomposition suggests that if race is more important in suburban than central city labor markets it could limit the potential employment gains made by blacks from having a suburban residential location. In this next section, I examine the relative importance of race and "space" in Prince George's to examine this argument in detail.

Table 5.12 shows the contribution of treatment (race) and residential location (space) in Prince George's to the racial employment rate differences in the PGDC area. The figures under the racial employment rate difference column were determined by adding the treatment and endowment effects of the residential location-education interacted variables for Prince George's given in the decomposition analysis found in Tables 5.10 and 5.11.

I also include the results of a partial decomposition analysis of these same variables comparison. Given this method, in the case of blacks for example, to estimate the endowment effect, whites are placed in the black world (endowments), or, more specifically, whites' interacted Prince George's-education variable means (endowments) are placed in the black, interacted residential location-education models shown in Table 5.9:

$$\hat{E}_B = \hat{a}_B + \hat{b}_B \, \overline{X}_B + \hat{c}_B \, \overline{PG}_W \tag{5.3}$$

where B and W refer to the black and white samples, respectively. On the other hand, to estimate the treatment effect, blacks are placed in the white world (treatment), or blacks' interacted Prince George's-education variable means are placed in the white, interacted residential location-education models.

The first row of the table shows the actual white-black and white-Latino employment rate differences of .16 and .11, respectively, in the PGDC area shown in Table 5.8. Given the Oaxaca and Blinder method discussed above, if blacks and Latinos were given the same endowments as whites for the interacted residential location-education variables in PG (this is also equivalent to giving blacks and Latinos the white residential location endowment in Prince George's—.80), the racial employment rate differences would decrease to .06 and .02, respectively. Thus, this endowment difference between whites' and blacks' interacted PG-education variables explains 63 and 81 percent of the white-black and white-Latino employment rate gap, respectively, in the PGDC area. It is clear, then, that the combined effect of living in the suburbs with job availability and going to PG schools does indeed matter and that whites' bigger endowment in these factors widens the racial employment rate differences as the spatial mismatch suggests. On the other hand, if blacks and Latinos were treated the same as whites in PG's labor market, the racial employment rate differences would decrease to .08 and .04, respectively. This treatment effect explains 50 and 63 percent of the white-black and white-Latino employment rate gap, respectively, in the PGDC area. It is also clear, then, that race is also important, and that the negative treatment of blacks and Latinos in PG's labor markets causes blacks and Latinos to fall further behind their white counterparts in labor market outcomes in the suburbs as compared to the central city.

The table also shows that under the Oaxaca and Blinder method the treatment (race) of blacks and Latinos in PGIB is more important than the endowment effect (space), and the endowment effect in PGOB is more important than the treatment effect in explaining the racial

The Confounding Influence of Race in Space 129

difference in employment in the PGDC area. As noted earlier, these results are interesting since one should expect blacks and Latinos in PGIB to be equally as well off as or better off than their white counterparts in employment since a higher concentration of blacks and Latinos in the PGDC area live in PGIB relative to their white counterparts, since a greater proportion of blacks and Latinos in the PGDC area live in PGIB with high school degrees than their white counterparts, and since PGIB contains the majority of the county's jobs.

The results of the partial decomposition method show that the treatment effect (race) is as important as the endowment effect (space) in the residential-education interacted variables in PG, and its two sub-areas, and explains more of the racial employment rate differences in the PGDC area. If blacks were treated in the same way as whites in PG's labor market, the white-black employment rate difference in the PGDC area would fall to .02. Thus, this treatment effect in PG explains 88 percent of this employment rate difference. On the other hand, if blacks had the same residential location-education endowments in PG as whites, the racial employment rate difference would fall to .10, and this effect would only explain 38 percent of the employment difference between these groups in the PGDC area. In the case of Latinos, if they were treated in the same way as whites in PG's labor market, the white-Latino employment rate in the PGDC area would disappear and Latinos' employment rate would be 3 percentage points higher than that of whites. At the same time, if Latinos had the same residential location-education endowments in PG as whites, the racial employment rate difference would also disappear.

The fact that the treatment effect is much stronger than the endowment effect in the partial decomposition than in the Oaxaca and Blinder method is primarily due to the fact that racial groups means and coefficients are differenced in the latter decomposition method, while they are not in partial method. It is not clear to me which of these methods is more accurate. However, it would not be unreasonable to conclude that the true endowment (space) and treatment (race) effects may fall somewhere in between these two methods. If this is true, then it is very likely that the treatment effect (race) is not just as important, but more important than the endowment effect (space).

CONCLUSION

I have explored the labor market outcomes of young males in the District of Columbia and Prince George's County, Maryland areas. The results of this chapter like those in the previous chapter show that both race and space are important determinants of racial differences in youth labor markets. In this chapter, however, we took into account black suburbanization patterns that likely biased the results in chapter 3 against the spatial mismatch hypothesis. Given that labor market opportunities appear to be better in Prince George's than in DC, it is not surprising that young males labor market outcomes in Prince George's are better than those of their DC counterparts, as the spatial mismatch hypothesis suggests. However, the differences in labor market outcomes between the two areas are more striking for young white than either young black or Latino males, suggesting that young white males benefit more from a suburban residential location than do their young black or Latino male counterparts. In fact, young black and Latino males' measures of economic welfare are worse in relation to their white male counterparts in Prince George's than in DC. These results imply that racial discrimination against black and Latino youth in the labor market appears more intense in the suburbs than in the central city.

Part of this sharp racial divergence in labor market outcomes in Prince George's as compared to DC stems from greater proportions of whites living in the 'outer beltway' of Prince George's and who either go to, or attended, with or with out a high school degree, schools here than either their black or Latino counterparts. These youth are more likely to do better in the labor market not only because of their greater concentration of human capital stock in the 'outer beltway' of Prince George's, particularly in high school degrees, but also because these schools may be perceived to be better than others in the area by employers. But if this were true, we would also expect black and Latino youth do to well in 'outer beltway' labor markets since it is also assumed that they either go to or attended schools here as well. This is not the case, however, since only those black and Latino youth with high school degrees in the 'outer beltway' do better in the labor market than their DC enrolled-in-school counterparts. What this suggests is that, as Kirschenman and Neckerman (1991) point out, whites from the suburbs are the most preferred by employers and are most likely to get jobs. Employment probabilities of black and Latino youth from the

The Confounding Influence of Race in Space 131

same distant suburbs are much lower than their white counterparts. These youth may need a high school diploma to get employed here since employers may be suspicious of their productivity or trainability.

The increasing intensity of racial discrimination in Prince George's confounds the importance of having a suburban residential location on employemnt. While whites endowment advantage in having a Prince George's residence explains between 38 and 63 percent of the white-black employment rate difference in the prince George's-Washington, DC area and between 81 percent and all of the Latino-white employment rate difference in this area, race explains between 50 and 88 percent of the white-black employment rate difference and between 63 percent and all of the white-Latino employment rate difference in this area.

The most interesting results are found in the 'inner beltway' of Prince George's. This areas houses the majority of the suburban county's jobs and has been responsible for most of the county's job growth. In addition, a greater concentration of blacks live in this area. And, in the sample, a greater proportion of blacks and Latinos with high school degrees live in this area in relation to their white counterparts. The combination of these factors suggests that blacks and Latinos should do as well as or better than their white counterparts in the labor market. However, the decomposition results show that although blacks and Latinos, in general, do have a residential endowment advantage over their white counterparts in this area at every educational level, the treatment of blacks and Latinos in this area effectively wipes out any employment advantages they may have had over their white counterparts.

These results shed interesting light on the demand side of Kain's third hypothesis. Kain argued that the suburbanization of jobs would probably reduce suburban employers' willingness to hire black workers because many suburban firms feared that importing black workers into white suburbs would offend white residents. Of course, when Kain presented this argument in the 1960s there were relatively few blacks living in the suburbs. However, Prince George's is a case in point where blacks have managed to penetrate the suburbs in large numbers to the extent that they represent a majority of the county by 1990. Yet, employers there still seem hesitant to hire blacks at the same rate as whites. However, where the hire rate of blacks is greatest in the suburbs is precisely where they represent the numerical majority, in the 'inner beltway' of Prince George's. Let us then examine this area more closely.

Young black and Latino males tend to do worse in the labor market relative to their white counterparts in the 'outer beltway' of Prince George's as opposed to the 'inner beltway' or DC. In fact, the black/white employment rate ratio is .80, .83, and .51 in DC, the 'inner beltway' and the 'outer beltway' areas, respectively. At the same time, in 1990, blacks made up 70, 64 and 37.0 percent of DC's, the 'inner beltway' and "outer beltway's" population (*US Census* 1994). What this suggests is that where there is a numerically dominant black population, blacks tend to do better relative to their white counterparts than in areas where there is not a numerically dominant black population. The success of blacks in the labor market not only hinges on the availability of jobs where blacks live, but also on the concentration of blacks relative to whites in an area. The consumer discrimination that Kain suggested occurred in the suburbs in the 1960s and which prevented employers from hiring blacks, may be buffered by the presence of blacks. However, we should still expect hostility and consumer discrimination to be stronger in suburban areas that have fewer blacks.

In fact, this hypothesis is supported by recent research on hiring in the DC area using audit analysis. Bendick, Jr. et al. (1994), using matched pairs of minority and white research assistants posing as applicants for the same jobs in the Washington, DC labor market, found that black applicants were treated less favorably than their equally qualified white counterparts more than one-fifth of the time. Latino applicants were treated less favorably than their equally qualified white counterparts a little less than one-fifth of the time. In addition, in comparison to DC, this mistreatment was a little more severe in the closer Maryland suburbs of DC and a lot more severe in the farther Virginia suburbs where there are fewer blacks.

Most research suggests that as the percentage of blacks in an area rises the likelihood of whites having a job increases (Farley 1987). This is precisely what we found in chapter 4 with a slight caveat: that such white advantage in the labor market disappears when blacks become the numerically dominant group in an area. In other words, this "white gains" hypothesis suggests that whites become more preferred in hiring by employers as the number of blacks in the area increases. The implication of this is that employers may be less likely to hire blacks because they are uncertain about their characteristics. Given this theory, we should expect to find blacks performing worse in the labor market relative to their white counterparts in DC and the 'inner beltway' rather than in the 'outer beltway', since the percentage of blacks in an area is greater in the former areas than the latter.

There are two basic propositions that may explain why blacks do not perform worse in the labor market relative to their white counterparts in DC and the 'inner beltway' than in the 'outer beltway'. First, the "sheltered workplace hypothesis" suggests that blacks may not be penalized in hiring in certain areas. According to this hypothesis, blacks encounter less consumer discrimination in areas where there are many blacks in relation to whites simply because the consumers are more likely to be black. Second, Osterman (1980) suggests that in areas where there is a numerically dominant black population, that population may place pressure on firms to hire blacks. Moreover, this pressure may be sufficient to neutralize or dominate the "white gains" effect mentioned above. Thus, blacks' consumer strength may prevent consumer discrimination from taking place in DC and the 'inner beltway' in a way that it might have taken place if blacks did not make up a numerically dominant population. Moreover, this pressure may also benefit young Latino males in the same way that it may benefit young black males. But since racial differences exist in employment outcomes even in the most ideal situation for blacks, i.e., the 'inner beltway', the pressure that a numerically dominant black population can put on employers to hire blacks may still not be enough to negate employers' uncertainties of hiring, and, possibly, negative attitudes towards, black workers. Like the story in chapter 4, there may exist, then, a critical threshold under which the numbers of blacks in an area relative to those of whites may lead to white gains, and over which the numbers of blacks in an area relative to those of whites may lead to the neutralization or minimization of these gains. Although blacks make up a fair amount of the 'outer beltway' population of Prince George's, they may not have the numbers to neutralize this white gains effect.

The experiments here suggest that residential location does matter, but it matters more for young white males than it does for either young black or Latino males. In Prince George's, particularly in the 'inner beltway' where labor market opportunities appear better for young black males than in DC, young white males are still more likely to have a job than either young black or Latino males controlling for personal and family background characteristics. Employment discrimination against blacks and Latinos in Prince George's, then, may explain part of the reason why young black and Latino males do not make up any ground in the labor market in relation to whites by having a residential location in Prince George's. Thus, although residential location in the suburbs improves young black and Latino males' likelihood of having a job compared to their counterparts in DC, the confounding influence of race over space appears to severely limit the potential magnitude of this improvement. These results suggest that previous and future studies of race and space could be misleading since the positive effects of moving to the suburbs are offset by the negative effects of increasing discrimination there. Thus, unless researchers control adequately for these two effects, the estimated, positive coefficients of a suburban location are likely understated if racial discrimination there is high.

CHAPTER 6
The Case for Preserving Targeted Policy Approaches to Ease the Employment Difficulties of Minority Youth

SPACE OR RACE?

The intention of this study was to gain more clarity on the relative importance of space and race as causes of racial differences in youth employment. Given the analysis shown here, I have found that, after controlling for personal and family characteristics and the suburbanizaiton patterns of blacks, race, or how blacks and Latinos are treated in the labor market, and space, or the residential locations of youth, are equal and important determinants of young blacks' and Latinos' low employment levels. In fact, in the case study of the Washington, DC area, race and space account for almost all of the racial differences in employment rates among young men.

Although race is an important factor in employment across metropolitan areas generally, the evidence shown here indicates that racial discrimination is more important in suburban than central city labor markets for youth. A central argument in this book is that increased racial discrimination in hiring in the suburbs may explain minority youth's employment difficulties and may be a reason why space might matter in metropolitan labor markets. Most scholars are quick to indict space as a cause of minority youth's lower employment when lower employment rates are observed for central city, minority youth. However, space to these scholars usually means only the problem of physical access to jobs. Jobs, particularly low-skilled ones, continue to move from central cities to suburbs. In addition, there is a tremendous literature that documents significant housing market discrimination against minorities that limits their housing choices and constrains their residential locations to central cities. Given this emerging spatial mismatch between the location of jobs and minority residential locations, it is quite plausible to explain the lower employment rates of central city, minority youth as a function of spatial frictions that are represented by physical job access problems. However, the evidence in this book reveals that though there are differences across residential areas in the employment of youth, indicating that spatial cleavages in labor markets do matter, the precise mechanism that makes space matter is put into serious question. And this question is most relevant in the case of minority youth.

How might space matter? On the one hand, the most obvious mechanism that might explain why space matters is the increased commute and search costs that central city, minority youth must pay to attain abundant, yet distant suburban jobs. These increased costs, such as longer commuting times to work and increased monetary costs for gas and/or bus fare, may make such suburban jobs less attractive to central city youth. Thus, spatial frictions likely cause blacks and other minorities in central cities not to look for or commute to work in suburbs. Such youth are likely to search for work exclusively in central cities where job opportunities have diminished profoundly since the 1960s thereby driving their joblessness upwards. On the other hand, greater employment discrimination against blacks and other minority groups in suburbs may also limit blacks' access to jobs. That is, even if blacks and other minority youth overcome the problem of physical access to jobs and get to the suburban employment door, they may not be let in as a result of employment discrimination.

This study suggests that both of these explanations about why space might matter are equally plausible, but it gives no indication of when either explanation might be more important. Thus, this research suggest that researchers should not be so quick to blame the higher jobless rates of minority youth on problems of physical distance to jobs if space is found to matter in labor markets. This is because the social problem of race in suburban labor markets is also likely to cause spatial problems for minority youth seeking work. In the case study of the Washington, DC area, the analysis revealed that if black and Latino youth lived in areas with greater job opportunities thus increasing their physical access to jobs, their employment rates did rise by fairly substantial amounts. However, if similar white youth lived in such areas, their employment rate rose by substantially greater amounts, suggesting that white youth receive a greater employment premium than minority youth as a result of living in job-rich areas. This is likely true because greater degrees of racial discrimination in suburban as opposed to central city areas limited the potential employment gains to be gotten by blacks as a result of having a suburban residential location. Moreover, the analysis also revealed that if blacks were treated the same as whites in these suburban, job-rich areas regardless if more minority youth moved to these areas, their employment rates rose by equal amounts as well. Thus, both physical distance and greater degrees of racial discrimination in suburban labor markets are key mechanisms that make space matter in youth labor markets. As we will explore momentarily, these findings are important for policy interventions. If we find that race does indeed matter in youth labor markets, interventions in the labor market that are aimed only at reducing the spatial problem of physical accessibility to jobs will likely fail.

My sense is, then, that the way in which black and Latino youth are treated in the labor market is a constant theme in the story of their labor market difficulties, and that other factors that are related to space, such as the extent of job decentralization in metropolitan areas or whether or not one has a suburban residential location, seem to intensify or mitigate the employment barriers faced by these groups. As such, it is extremely important, I contend, that targeted policies for assisting black and Latino youth in the labor market must be preserved and strengthened first before building universal measures into such policies if we are to eliminate racial differences in labor market outcomes for young adults in metropolitan areas. In addition, equal emphasis should be placed on policies to combat racial discrimination in labor markets and on policies that attempt to solve the problem of physical distance in urban labor markets if we are to solve the minority youth employment problem.

WHEN MIGHT RACE MATTER?

The evidence gathered in this book not only suggests that race is important in labor markets and is as important as space, it also provides some clues about when and under what conditions it might matter in labor markets. The study reveals structural factors contribute to when race might matter in labor markets. The structural factors include the percentage of blacks in a particular area and the availability of jobs in that area.

A key structural factor that could influence when race might matter in labor markets is the level and presence of the black population in a particular area, be it in the central city or suburb. If the presence of blacks in an particular area is high but not high enough to make them a numerically dominant group, then discrimination against blacks in labor markets might become more intense than if they made up a small percentage of that area. The source of this discrimination could come from white consumers, employers, or employees. Moreover, the source of discrimination is in some way dependent upon the type of industries that are found in the particular area. For example, if a particular suburb has many retail stores where consumer/employee contact is very direct, then consumer discrimination might be more important than either employer or employee discrimination. Nonetheless, race might matter in labor markets when the percentage of blacks in an area is large. Given this circumstance, whites may feel that their jobs or well-being are threatened by a growing black presence, and therefore may take measures to limit competition for jobs by creating barriers to black employment.

However, the ability of whites to effectively erect or maintain such barriers to black employment is contingent on the level of blacks in the particular area. If blacks are the numerically dominant population group in a particular area, whites' ability to erect or maintain such barriers to black employment is considerably compromised. That is, if blacks become the majority of a particular area, they could as a result of their sheer numbers neutralize whites' ability to erect barriers to black employment. For example, there may be less consumer and employee discrimination against blacks since blacks presumably make up more of the consumers and employees in the area than if they were not the majority group. Likewise, since blacks are the numerically dominant group, they could put pressure on local employers to hire black workers if the source of discrimination came from employers.

The findings in this book are entirely consistent with this story. The case study in chapter 5 shows that young black and Latino males tend to do worse in the labor market relative to their white counterparts in the 'outer beltway' of Prince George's as opposed to the 'inner beltway' and DC. In 1990, the black/white employment rate ratio was

.80, .83, and .51 in DC, the 'inner beltway' and 'outer beltway' of Prince George's, respectively. At the same time, blacks made up 70, 64, 37 percent of DC's, the 'inner beltway' and 'outer beltway' population, respectively (*US Census* 1994). These results suggests as in areas where blacks represent a substantial proportion of the population but not the majority group, they are likely to face greater degrees of racial discrimination in employment. In addition, the results in chapter 4 also support this story. The evidence there showed that whites' jobless durations were shorter the larger the fraction of blacks in the labor market. However, when blacks became the dominant group in the labor force, whites' jobless duration were wholly unaffected by the proportion of blacks in the area.

The extent of employment discrimination against blacks as a function of the size of black populations in an area may also be conditional on the availability of jobs. If the level of aggregate demand in an area is low, i.e., limited job availability, then there are fewer jobs to go around. Given this condition, whites may be more inclined to adopt measures to limit competition for these jobs irrespective of whether they are the numerical dominant group in a particular area. Again, in this case, discrimination in any form, i.e., employee, employer, or consumer discrimination, against blacks in the labor market might become more intense. Moreover, the practice of statistical discrimination by employers might become more intense against blacks as well because employers have more workers to chose from during hiring. The evidence in chapter 4 seems to support these claims. Whites' jobless durations were not affected by the local unemployment rate, while those of blacks and Latinos were. Blacks' and Latinos' jobless durations were considerably longer as the unemployment rate rose.

UNIVERSAL OR TARGETED POLICIES?

In policy circles, there is considerable debate concerning the merits of moving towards more universal approaches to social policy and away from targeted approaches to address social problems, particularly those regarding race. In general, universal policy approaches attempt to build social policy for broad constituencies, including groups of all income categories and racial backgrounds, while targeted policy approaches attempt to direct social policy to specific groups whose social or economic problems are deemed worthy of policy consideration.

Policies to achieve full employment, either through fiscal or monetary manipulations of the economy, may be considered a universal policy approach since the effects of such a policy can be felt by many groups of people, while affirmative action policies may be considered targeted policies since they are intended to affect a specific group of individuals.

The proponents of universal policy approaches claim that targeted policy approaches are doomed to failure because of two fundamental reasons. First, they claim that targeted policy approaches are more likely to loose political support because they have a small constituent base (Skocpol 1991; Wilson 1987). Policies that target specific income groups, for example, are likely to loose support from taxpayers, particularly those that may be slightly above the income cutoff. These groups, consequently, may not benefit from such policies, but their problems may be fundamentally no different than those who do benefit. Second, policies that target specific groups are likely to lose political support from those who are not members of the targeted groups. Moreover, it is also argued that all members of a targeted group may not receive benefits of policies targeted to that group. For example, Wilson (1987) claims that race-specific, targeted policies benefit middle-class members of the group while hurting those of that group who are poor. This point is highly contentious and controversial because it suggests that the social and economic mobility of a targeted group is a zero-sum game. For example, if the black middle-class gains from a particular targeted policy towards blacks, then according to this reasoning the black poor must lose. This is a faulty interpretation since other intervening factors may be related to or cause black middle-class' upward mobility rather than a particular targeted policy itself.

On the other hand, it is argued that universal programs, by definition, do not have the qualities of targeted programs, and are therefore less likely to lose political support. These programs are broad based and inclusive, it is argued, and are more likely to be successful in improving the lot of the poor and in mitigating the social and economic problems of certain groups because they receive broad political support. Further, it is argued that the relative success of social policies in countries like Canada, Sweden, and German stems from the fact that they have more universality built into their policy regimes.

While many of these arguments are likely true, the criticisms leveled against targeted policies are likely overstated. There are other factors besides whether the policy approach is universal or targeted that can influence political support for such programs. Targeted programs, for example, are more likely to be supported politically when these programs are linked to work (Greenstein 1991). In addition, the health of the government budgets also affect whether or not such policies are supported. Targeted policies, then, can be supported politically if they are designed carefully.

Additionally, there are potential problem with universal policy approaches as well. First, pushing for universal policy approaches can produce unintended negative effects. If certain groups are systematically affected differentially by universal polices than other groups, social or economic gaps between such groups can develop, persist or grow. Second, universal programs are expensive. Universal programs do have a broader base and perhaps a stronger constituency, and they may even be less stigmatizing than targeted approaches, but advocates of universal policy approaches do not adequately deal with the reality of fiscal constraints (Sawhill 1989). In addition to the redesigning of policy, universal programs require massive social spending. Under periods of fiscal constraint, the introduction of new major policy approach proposals are likely to fail because taxpayers are not willing to shoulder the financial burden of these proposals. Third, the introduction of universal policy proposals may provide an incentive for policy makers opposed to targeted programs to dismantle them out without any guarantee that successful universal policy approaches will be implemented. Pushing for universality in periods of fiscal constraint and budget cuts by conservative governments, then, could further reinforce racial inequality and hurt the poor.

The research shown here suggests that some of the problems with universal policies are likely true and may reinforce racial inequality in youth labor markets. In the case of young men, universal employment programs, for example, may benefit white youth more than either black or Latino youth because such programs, by definition, do not adequately tackle the problem of race in labor markets. The lessons learned from universal programs come from countries that are fairly racially homogenous, e.g., Sweden and Germany. It is unclear, then, how countries with heterogeneous populations will fare under strictly universal programs. Some universal programs in the US have been greatly successful, such as Social Security, and have benefited racial groups equally. However, such programs presume employment since in order to receive social Security one must have worked. But what of getting jobs?

Advocates of universality make the implicit assumption that race is no longer significant in determining social and economic outcomes. If race, however, is still significant, as this study documents, it is likely that the same mechanisms that can produce unequal racial outcomes in society can also produce unequal results under universal programs. Those who are discriminated against in society may receive unequal access to or information about universal programs, and they may be treated more poorly than others in these programs, thereby limiting the program's effectiveness. Universal programs, then, while they may, in general, lift the boats of those who experience social and economic problems in society, may lift some boats higher than others.

Given the extreme racial differences in youth employment documented in this study and the persistent problem of race in youth labor markets, it is reasonable to suggest that targeted programs need be protected, re-thought, and strengthened first, and then attempts to build in universal measures into these policies should be made since universal programs have greater potential downsides than targeted measures. This approach will ensure some basic protection of minority youth in the labor market and will likely minimize racial inequality in labor market outcomes.

THE APPROPRIATE POLICY MIX

The results of this study document that there are racial differences in the factors that cause youth joblessness. As such, policy prescriptions need be tailored to the specific problems faced by different racial groups in the labor market if we are to have any impact on reducing racial differences in youth employment. The basic results suggest that young white males tend to do much better in the labor market than young black and Latino males in both the central city and suburbs. In addition, young males tend to do worse in the central city relative to their suburban counterparts. Since the labor market opportunities are very poor for young black, and to a certain extent Latino, males with limited education, it is clear that policies directed at the institutional, supply-, and demand-side of the labor market must be considered.

Institutional Responses

Race and space are important factors in labor markets for young male adults. Employers engage in statistical discrimination not simply because they have "bad" tastes for blacks or Latinos, but because they perceive these groups as having "uncertain productivities." To employers, hiring members from groups with "uncertain productivities" means encountering individuals with unpredictable training costs. It appears that employers seem to have no strategy to determine an unproductive from an productive black or Latino worker, and simply avoid hiring members from these groups altogether. But this hiring pattern generally results in the periodic rejection of well-qualified blacks and Latinos, and the systematic denial of job opportunities of minorities with low-skill or educaiton. Thus, it is clear from the results in this study that anti-discrimination efforts in labor markets must be enforced more heavily. These efforts should not only be directed at large firms, usually regulated by the Office of Federal Contract Compliance (OFCC), but also at small business, usually regulated by the Equal Employment Opportunity Commission. However, past efforts at this type of enforcement have not been very fruitful (Jencks 1992). Thus, policy-makers need to re-think the ways in which successful anti-discrimination regulation can take place.

Since efforts to eliminate discrimination in hiring have not been very successful, other indirect methods of addressing discrimination must be explored. First, statistical discrimination hiring could be reduced if support was given to local training organizations or agencies that developed relationships with local employers. Employers would be more likely to hire young black and Latino males if they had more information on the kinds of skills they possess. Young black and Latino males with certificates from such training organizations or agencies that employers respect and have worked with may decrease the kind of statistical discrimination that takes place in hiring. Thus, more support could be given to Community Development Corporations (CDC's) and other community based organizations or agencies (CBO's) that are engaged in employment and training. Many of these CDC's and CBO's are located in black and Latino communities. Harrison (1995) has shown that CDC's and CBO's are very involved in employment and training at the local level. These organizations develop relationships with employers to identify particular skill needs of local companies. These organizations, in turn, train workers in these skills by either contracting training out to other agencies or by providing this training themselves. In addition, they provide start-up assistance for local community enterprises which create more local jobs. Thus, skill training, job placement, and job creation activities are carried out simultaneously by these organizations. Most importantly, though,

CDC's and CBO's are successful in placing workers because employers are sure about what kind of labor they are getting. The increased employer certainty of workers is based on the successful track record of placed workers in firms.

Of course, one possible negative consequence of embedding local employment and training efforts in social capital relationships with firms is that those youth who do not posses certificates may become even less attractive to employers. Thus, even with such employment and training efforts, anti-discrimination enforcement must be a consistent policy response in youth labor markets to ensure equal treatment of minority youth worker.

If employers are less likely to hire young black and Latino males because they have had "bad" experiences with them in the past and, if as Kirshenman and Neckerman (1991) have suggested, cultural differences between young black males and white employers negatively impacts the hiring of minority youth, it may be important for states or local governments to provide "diversity training" to local small and medium sized business. The goal of this training would be to sensitize managers to cultural differences, so that managers can deconstruct appearances from objective measures of skill and ability.

Demand-Side Responses

Certainly, the availability of jobs does matter in increasing black and Latino youth's access to jobs. However, even with a full employment economy, racial differences in youth employment rates are not eliminated (Freeman 1991). Nonetheless, job creation strategies should help to increase the employment level of blacks and Latinos, particularly in the central city, although these strategies should be targeted to these groups in the suburbs as well. Subsidized job creation programs in the public or private sectors such as the demonstration projects under the Youth Demonstration Act of 1977 (e.g., Youth Incentive Enrollment Pilot Projects), and Job Corps have been effective in increasing young adult employment (Betsey et al. 1985; Farkas et al. 1983). In fact, the Youth Incentive Enrollment Projects were successful in eliminating employment differences between young whites and blacks. These programs also placed youth in meaningful jobs. However, because of inadequate funding and program design, we know little about how successful these programs were in the long run or how well these program participants performed in the labor market after exit. What we do know about Job Corps is that work experience alone did not appear to improve employability of youth, that work experience is more effective with skill training and placement services and that skill training is ineffective without demand-side, job creation strategies (Bassi and Ashenfelter 1986).

Job creation strategies can also include place-based strategies. The most dominant placed-based job strategy in the past decade has been enterprise zones under the Reagan and Bush administrations, and empowerment zones under the Clinton administration. Enterprise zone strategies used tax and other financial incentives such as job creation and wage credits, employer income tax credits, selective hiring credits, and investment and property tax credits to encourage firms to locate or expand in particular zones, usually in parts of distressed urban communities (Erickson and Friedman 1991). The goal of enterprise zones was to provide incentives to firms or business to locate in distressed areas in order to increase the number of jobs and spur economic development in such areas (Green 1991).

The results of enterprise zones has been somewhat mixed. The major criticism of such policies is that they do not generate new jobs, just induce firms to move from one location of a metropolitan area to another. In fact, Ladd (1994) found that in England, where enterprise zones were originally conceived, the main effect of such policies was to relocate firms to the zones from nearby locations. However, if the goal of such a policy is to increase minority youth employment and if the location of jobs into black and Latino communities from other communities can reduce the negative effect of discrimination and narrow racial employment differences, the potential negative effects of such polices may in fact be positive.

Second, firms that locate in enterprise zones may not hire residents in or near the zone because they may not possess the required skills. Thus, the wage rate subsidies given to employers as part of the enterprise zone package may not have been sufficient to overcome employers' resistance to hiring residents as workers. Given these problems, Clinton's empowerment zone policies reflect some learning of past problems and have included more community-building components. However, it remains to be seen whether or not this new program, with bigger zone areas and greater emphasis on improving the social environment, will do any better. The recommendation of continuing these new zone strategies is contingent upon their ability to provide local residents with jobs.

Once targeted demand-side policies have been secured, more universal measures can be introduced. The most relevant universal demand-side strategy involves full employment polices. However, as I mentioned earlier, these policies by themselves, while increasing the employment levels of blacks and Latinos, may not eliminate racial differences in employment. Nonetheless, fiscal and monetary policies designed to stimulate aggregate demand are important to raise employment levels of young adults, particularly black and Latino youth in the central city, so long as inflationary pressures are contained. But not all fiscal and monetary policies will have an equally positive impact on youth employment, particularly those who are low skilled. For example, lower interest rates through expansionary monetary policy may not stimulate investment in distressed communities where investment is most needed. Likewise, fiscal stimulus through tax cuts may have little impact on these distressed communities because the disposable incomes of low-income households are unlikely to be affected by reducing taxes (Bluestone et al. 1994). This is precisely why fiscal stimulus through youth jobs programs, and possibly even infrastructure development in distressed communities, would have a greater impact on youth employability than just general fiscal policies.

Supply-Side Responses

It is unquestionable that educational attainment, particularly the receipt of a high school degree, improves the employability minority youth. Young black males without a high school degree are penalized in the labor market compared to others because employers may be uncertain about their productivity or trainability. Although efforts should be made to increase the educational attainment of black and Latino youth, efforts must also be taken to ensure that black and Latino youth do not have to possess more educational attainment than their white counterparts to be competitive with these youth for jobs.

Policies to help reduce the high school drop-out rate would address the goal of increasing minority youth's educational attainment. It is critical that efforts be made to reach young black and Latino men in school before they enter high school and decide to drop-out. Expanding Headstart programs for elementary students and Outward Bound programs for junior high and high school students may help in this regard. Within the high school system, public high schools, where the majority of blacks and Latinos attend, must be improved by improving

The Case for Preserving Targeted Policy Approaches 147

teacher quality and by changing the differential way in which blacks and Latinos are taught in school (Jaynes and Williams 1989). Moreover, measures must be taken to ensure adequate funding levels of public schools. Finally, efforts must be made to develop remedial education for students who fall below their grade level.

Job training to increase the skills of young adults may also increase their employability. Support of existing federal training programs such as JTPA should continue, and more support should be given to CDC's and CBO's as employer trainers.

The development of youth apprenticeship programs also have the potential to increase the skills and employability of youth. These programs are more universal in nature since they apply to young people in general, particularly those who are not college bound. Efforts must be made to ensure the participation of black and Latino youth in these programs and ensure that their training levels and that the kinds of training that they receive are no different from those of comparable whites.

The shell of youth apprenticeship programs are found in the 1990 Perkins Vocational Education Act, and, more specifically, in Clinton's School-To-Work Opportunities Act of 1993. The latter act proposed to bring together partnerships of employers, educators and others to build a high quality school-to-work system at the local level that intends to prepare young people for successful careers. The program is jointly administered by the Department of Education and Labor (U.S. Dept. of Labor and Education 1993).

The German experience is the most frequently cited model for an apprenticeship system. German students begin exploring occupations in the 7th grade, when many are tracked toward either a university or academic-technical program. By age 16, the latter group begins spending as many as four days a week on a worksite learning such skills as bookkeeping, electrical engineering or auto mechanics. In exchange for on-the-job training, students receive stipends averaging $400 a month and take interim and final exams supervised by their employers. More than half of the apprentices remain with the firm where they are trained and a larger share spend their careers in the same occupation (Lerman and Pouncy 1990).

Inspired by Germany's "dual system", which places more than 60 percent of 16-year-olds in apprenticeships, youth apprenticeship projects have sprung up in some 20 states since 1990. Students will complete a Certificate of Initial Mastery in basic skills such as reading and math, and then at age 16 pursue either a traditional college prep track or a "technical and professional" track, which is expected to include substantial time on the job in the form of youth apprenticeships.

In the U.S., youth apprentices under existing plans make a three-to-four year commitment to a trade and an employer, spanning the last year or two of high school and the following two years. Their hours on the paid job might rise from twenty per week in year one to full-time in year four. In the classroom, teachers and employers teach reading, math and other courses using workplace applications. In addition, one or more technical courses are tailored to a specific trade. At the conclusion of the program, students graduate with a high school diploma, significant work experience, credits toward a two-year associate degree and some kind of certificate of trade mastery (Stoll 1993).

However, there are potential problems with such apprenticeship programs. First, apprenticeship programs may discourage youth from pursuing a four-year college degree. In the best of circumstances, youth apprenticeship programs would lead to a two-year associate's degree. But since most associates credits are not transferable to Bachelor of Arts programs, i.e., four-year college degree, and since work experience for credit is rarely accepted by colleges, a youth apprenticeship graduate would have difficulty obtaining a B.A. And despite assurances that the workbased learning track is not second class to college prep and will not restrict students' options, program designers are finding that occupationally specific courses crowd out such needed college courses as foreign languages.

Secondly, tracking is another concern in apprenticeship programs. Sorting students into two clearly defined and different paths could pose a significant problem. The question of tracking is compounded by the disproportionate presence of minority students in public high schools. Most, if not all, of the high schools participating in apprenticeship programs are public (CQ Researcher, 1992). Minority students are disproportionately represented in public high schools in urban schools and, according to *Workforce 2000*, will make up nearly 50% of the entering workforce by the year 2000.

Thus, the potential tracking problem that may entail from youth apprenticeship programs may tend to reproduce racial hierarchies. Given the already poor rate of college enrollment by minority public high school students, the presence of youth apprenticeship programs may further serve as a disincentive for minority youth to enter college and gain high-tech or professional skills. These issues must be taken into account if youth apprenticeship programs are to be an adopted strategy to improve youth's employment opportunities.

Relevant Spatial Policies

Relevant spatial policies must be adopted to increase the physical accessibility of jobs for youth, particularly those in the central cities. Suburban dispersal policies, such as the Department of Housing and Urban Development's Moving to Opportunity Program, may be helpful in mitigating the negative influences of space on employment. One of the implicit policy implications of the spatial mismatch hypothesis is to induce minority population dispersal to the suburbs. If blacks and Latinos can move closer to areas with jobs, their employment levels should rise. Kain (1985) advocated suburban minority population dispersal to improve their economic welfare. Moreover, he showed that such dispersal could occur without additional construction of low-income housing in the suburbs. The exclusion of blacks from the suburbs was primarily attributable to discrimination in suburban housing markets and not from unaffordable housing. Such dispersal is unlikely to be successful without policy intervention in housing markets to reduce housing discrimination.

However, suburban dispersal policies may not increase the employment levels of blacks and Latinos for two basic reasons. First, the increasing presence of blacks and Latinos in suburbs may cause whites to respond by moving farther out into the suburbs or to the exurbs. White fight from the central cities as blacks increasingly penetrated these areas has been well documented. It is unclear whether this pattern will repeat itself in the suburbs if blacks or Latinos increasingly move there. More importantly though, jobs may also follow whites as blacks and Latinos begin to move into these formerly white areas. Secondly, discrimination against blacks by suburban employers may become more intense as the number of blacks in suburbs increases such that the potential employment gains from a suburban residential location might be erased by such discrimination.

The Gautreax Program was a significant residential mobility policy implemented in the 1970s. This program assisted households in Chicago, primarily black families, in moving from public to private housing, from mostly poor to moderate income communities. Although all households originally lived in the central city, many households moved to the suburbs in predominantly white higher income neighborhoods, while the remainder of others simply moved within the central city (Rosenbaum and Popkin 1991).

Rosenbaum and Popkin (1991) found that suburban movers in the Gautreax Program had a 14 employment advantage over their central city movers, controlling for relevant characteristics. While these results do reveal that a suburban move may be a good thing for blacks in the program, it is unclear what the long term effects of this program might be since these households moved into predominantly white upper-income suburban areas where few blacks live. If these whites do not perceive blacks to be a threat, then these black suburban movers might not face employment discrimination by employers. However, given an increasing presence of blacks, whites might begin to view black suburban movers as threats. Employment discrimination against such blacks, then, might intensify. In addition, white flight and job flight might also occur.

A downside to residential mobility programs is that they might undermine the success of CDC's and CBO's in training and placing young blacks and Latinos in jobs and in job creation. Most CDC's and CBO's are located in the central city and serve mostly minority populations. Suburban dispersal programs may undermine CDC's and CBO's by weakening their clientele base and their administrative structures. This is critical because these organizations in minority communities may buffer the negative effect of employer discrimination against blacks and Latinos.

Non-residential based policies should be pursued to increase the direct, physical access of jobs for youth. Efforts should be made to make "reverse commuting" easier for youth. These policies, such as the Department of Housing and Urban Development's 'Bridges to Opportunity' program, involve improving public transportation systems to improve transportation efficiency, i.e., decreasing travel time of workers, by better connecting central city and suburban bus or rail routes, using van pools and subsidizing private and public commutes to work. Public transportation subsidies are also likely to be effective in this regard. Such policy options also include subsidizing private transportation, or providing incentives for car pooling. More research should be done, however, to determine the effectiveness of these kinds of policies.

Policies to improve job access should also include those which improve workers' information about job openings. Efforts should be made to develop "job banks" to inform job seekers of available jobs for which they are qualified in urban areas. It is unclear to what extent job information policies are effective. Again, more research needs to be conducted to determine the effectiveness of these kinds of job information policies.

Appendices

Table A3.1: NLSY Sample Size by Race and Residential Location: 1984

	White		Black		Latino		Total	
	Number	Percent	Number	Percent	Number	Percent	Number	Percent
C.C.	821	41.0	671	67.5	430	62.9	1922	52.2
SUB.	1181	59.0	323	32.5	254	37.1	1758	47.8
Total	2002	54.4	994	27.0	684	18.6	3680	100.0

Table A3.2: Industrial Distribution by Race and Residential Location: 1984 (most recent job)

	White		Black		Latino		Total	
	Cen. City	Suburb	Cen. City	Suburb	Cen. City	Suburb	Cen. City	Suburb
Agricul.	4.3	2.8	3.2	2.4	10.3	2.3	4.5	2.7
Mining	0.8	1.4	1.0	0.7	0.5	0.6	0.8	1.2
Construc.	10.2	13.9	10.3	10.7	5.1	7.6	9.9	12.6
Manufac.	30.4	27.0	31.5	20.7	28.4	26.2	30.3	25.5
Transpor.	6.3	5.4	4.0	6.7	5.9	8.2	6.1	5.9
Whole. Trad	3.4	4.0	4.9	3.0	3.0	7.0	3.4	4.1
Retail Trade	21.2	22.4	14.6	16.9	14.5	22.5	20.4	21.2
F.I.R.E.	1.2	2.0	0.7	3.1	2.3	3.2	1.3	2.4
Services	20.5	18.9	25.0	28.6	22.5	20.3	20.9	21.2
Pub. Admin.	1.9	2.3	4.9	7.3	7.6	2.0	2.4	3.4

Table A4.1: SMSA's in Duration Models

Akron. OH
Albuquerque, NM
Alexandria, LA
llentown-Bethlehem-Easton, PA-NJ
Amarillo, TX
Anaheim-Santa Ana-Garden Grove, CA   S
Ann Arbor, MI
Anniston, AL
Appleton-Oshkosh, WI
Asheville, NC
Athens, GA
Atlanta, GA   C
Atlantic City, NJ
Augusta, SA-SC
Austin, TX
Bakersfield, CA
Baltimore, MD
Beaumont-Port Arthur-Orange, TX
Bellingham, WA
Billings, MT
Binghamton, NY-PA   S
Birmingham, AL
Bismarck, ND
Bloomington, IN
Boston, MA
Bristol, CT
Brownsville-Harlingen-San Benito, TX   S
Bryan-College Station, TX
Buffalo, NY
Canton, OH
Charleston-North Charleston, SC   S
Charlotte-Gastonia, NC

Charlottesville, VA
Chicago, IL   C
Cincinnati, OH-KY-IN
Cleveland, OH
Colorado Springs, CO
Columbia, SC
Columbus, OH
Corpus Christi, TX
Dallas-Fort Worth, TX
Davenport-Rock Island-Moline, IA-IL
Dayton, OH
Daytona Beach, FL
Denver-Boulder, CO
Demoines, IA
Detroit, MI
Eau Claire, WI
El Paso, Tx
Elkhart, IN
Enid, OK
Erie, PA
Eugene, OR
Flint, MI
Florence, SC   S
Fort Lauderdale-Hollywood, FL
Fresno, CA
Gainesville, FL
Gary-East Chicago, IN
Grand Rapids, MI
Great Falls, MT
Greely, CO   S
Green Bay, WI
Greensboro-Winston Salem, NC
Greenville, SC
Harrisburg, PA

Hartford, CT
Houston, TX
Huntsville, AL
Indianapolis, IN
Iowa City, IA
Jackson, MS
Janesville-Beloit, WI
Jersey City, NJ
Johnson City-Bristol, TN-VA
Kansas City, MO-KS
Kenosha, WI
Killeen-Temple, TX
Knoxville, TN
Lafayette, LA   C
Lake Charles, LA   S
Lansing-East Lansing, MI
Laredo, TX
Las Cruces, NM
Las Vegas, NV
Lawton, OK
Lima, OH
Lincoln, NE
Little Rock, AR
Lorain-Elyria, OH   S
Los Angeles-Long Beach, CA
Lubbock, TX
Madison, WI
Manchester, NH   C
McAllen, TX   S
Memphis, TN-AR-MI
Miami, FL
Milwaukee, WI
Minneapolis-St. Paul, MN
Mobile, AL
Modesto, CA
Montgomery, AL
Muskegon, MI
Nashville-Davidson, TN
New Bedford, MA

New Britain, CT
New Haven, CT   S
New Orleans, LA
New York, NY-NJ
Newark, NJ
Norfolk-Virginia Beach, VA-NC
Odessa, TX
Oklahoma City, OK
Omaha, NE
Orlando, FL
Pascagoula-Moss Point, MI
Pensacola, FL
Peoria, IL
Philadelphia, PA-NJ
Phoenix, AZ
Pittsburgh, PA
Portland, OR-WA
Providence, RI   S
Provo-Orem, UT
Racine, WI
Reading, PA
Richmond, VA   C
Riverside-San Bernadino, CA
Roanoake, VA   S
Rochester, NY
Sacramento, CA
Saginaw, MI
St. Louis, MO-IL
Salt Lake City-Ogden, UT
San Diego, CA
San Francisco-Oakland, CA
San Jose, CA
Santa Rosa, CA
Savannah, GA
Seattle-Everett, WA
Sioux City, IA-NE   C
Sioux Falls, SD   S
Spokane, WA

Springfield, MO
Springfield-Holyoke, MA   S
State College, PA
Steubenville, OH   S
Stockton, CA
Syracuse, NY
Tacoma, WA   C
Tampa-St. Petersburg, FL
Texarkana, TX-AR
Topeka, KA
Trenton, NJ
Tulsa, OK   S

Vallejo-Napa, CA
Victoria, TX
Visalia-Tulare-Porterville, CA
Waco, TX
Washington, DC-MD-VA
Wheeling, WV-OH
Wichita, KA
Wichita Falls, TX   C
Williamsport, PA
Wilmington, DL-NJ-MD
Yakima, WA
Youngstown-Warren, OH

Note:
   S = suburbs only
   C = central city only

Appendices

A4.2: THEORETICAL MODEL FOR JOBLESS DURATION ANALYSIS

A simple job search model is used in which the optimal search strategy is to continue searching for work until one receives a wage offer that exceeds the reservation wage. The reservation wage equates the marginal benefits and marginal costs of additional search. The expected completed duration of unemployment is a function of two probabilities; 1) the probability of receiving a job offer; and, 2) the probability of accepting that job offer.

The re-employment probability, h(t), which is a function of the probabilities described above, is also known as the hazard or failure rate. The hazard rate, h(t), is the probability of exiting a state, i.e., leaving unemployment, in a time interval conditional on having arrived in that state at t:

$$h(t) = \frac{\text{Probability of exiting between times t and t} + \Delta t}{(t) \text{ (Probability of exiting after time t)}} \quad (A.1)$$

which is simplified as

$$h(t)\, dt = g(t)\, dt / (1 - G(t)) \quad (A.2)$$

where $g(t)\, dt$ is the probability of accepting a job between time t and t + dt, $(1 - G(t))$ is the probability of joblessness at time t, and t is the duration of the current spell of joblessness.[38] The survivor function can be obtained by integrating this equation:

$$1 - G(t) = \exp\left[-\int_0^t h(z)dz\right] \quad (A.3)$$

which implies the density function:

$$g(t) = h(t)\exp\left[-\int_0^t h(z)dz\right] \quad (A.4)$$

Following Kletzer (1992), I used a likelihood function that allowed estimation of the determinants of re-employment probabilities for workers using the survivor and density function. I selected those young adults who were not working at the start of the 1984 interview date. Then, I followed their weekly labor market experiences until the 1985 interview date and observed whether or not they had received employment during this period. For those who had received a job, I identified the exact week of their employment. Thus, the data set contains both completed and uncompleted, (i.e., censored data), spells of joblessness. Given the structure of this data, the appropriate form for the likelihood function is:

$$L = \prod_{i=1}^{NU} \left[\frac{1 - G_i(t_i + h_i)}{1 - g(t_i)} \right] x \prod_{j=1}^{NE} \left[\frac{g_j(t_j + w_j)}{1 - G(t_j)} \right] \quad (A.5)$$

where NU is the number of jobless observations at the beginning of the 1985 interview, t is the jobless duration at the beginning of the 1984 interview, h is the number of weeks between the two interviews, NE is the number of individuals who find a job by the beginning of the 1985 interview, and w is the number of weeks after the beginning of the 1984 interview before becoming employed. To operationalize this likelihood function, an appropriate functional form for G must be chosen. I assume that G follows a Weibull distribution, which is consistent with research on unemployment duration using hazard analysis (Lynch, 1989; Kletzer, 1992). The Weibull distribution is used in much of the unemployment duration analysis because it is assumed that the longer one stays in an unemployment state, the more likely that individual is to leave that state.[39] The survivor function, 1—G(t), for the Weibull is:

$$1 - G(t) = \exp(-\exp(X'B)t^a) \quad (A.6)$$

Thus, if an independent variable is associated with longer jobless durations its coefficient has a positive sign.

Appendices

Table A4.3: Maximum Likelihood Weibull Estimates of Jobless Durations for Central City Young White Males

Variable	Coefficient
Constant	-3.909***
	(1.152)
Age	0.021
	(0.044)
Highest Grade Completed	0.029
	(0.057)
Married	0.099
	(0.478)
Children	-0.568**
	(0.268)
Unemployment Compensation	0.782***
	(0.283)
Local Unemployment Rate	-0.019
	(0.031)
Job Decentralization	-0.010**
	(0.005)
% of CC L. F. Black (0–.10)	-0.321
	(0.235)
% of CC L.F. Black (.10–.20)	-0.214
	(.249)
% of CC L.F. Black (.35–.50)	0.465**
	(.207)
% of CC L.F. Black (>.50)	0.182
	(.394)
% of CC L. F. Latino	0.006
	(0.008)
Total Population (log)	0.004
	(0.008)
Log Likelihood	-295.51
Prob>chi2	0.03
N	174

Notes: std. errors in parenthesis; * significant at .10, ** significant at .05, *** significant at .01.

Figure A5.1
Washington, D.C. and Prince George's County Area

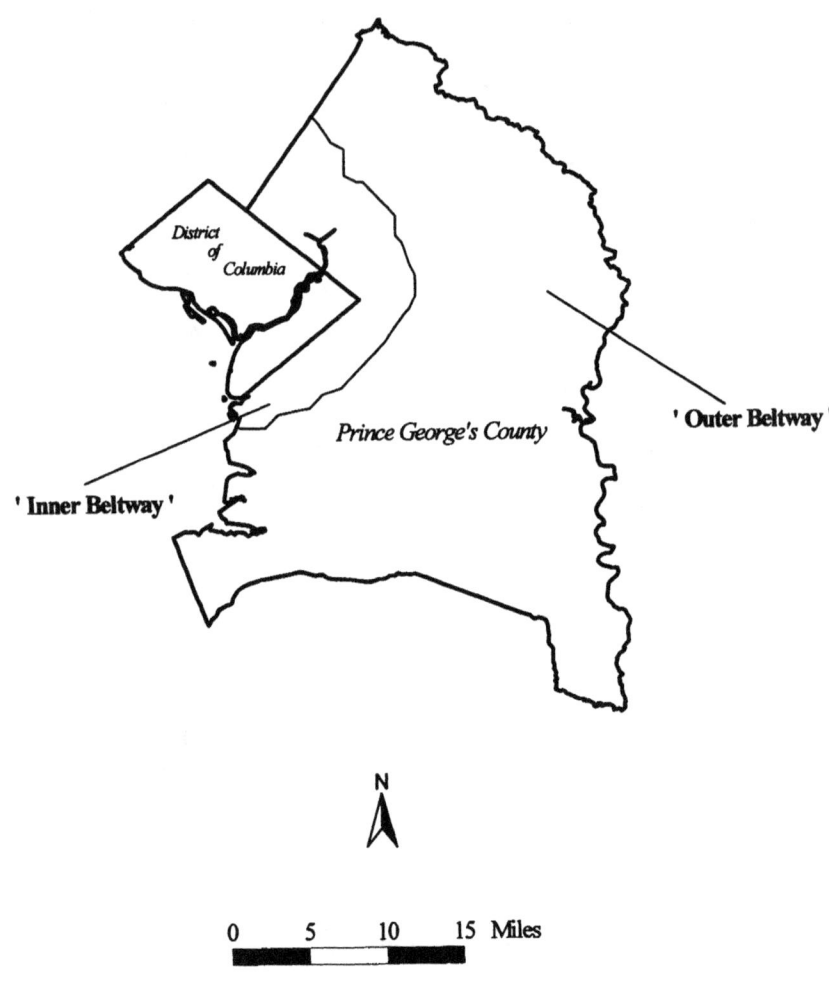

Table A5.1: 1990 Sample Size for White, Black, and Latino Youth Aged 16–21 in Washington, DC and Prince George's County, MD

	White		Black		Latino		Total	
	Number	Percent	Number	Percent	Number	Percent	Number	Percent
DC	145	20.0	707	52.1	185	46.5	1037	41.8
Prince George's County	580	80.0	653	48.9	209	52.5	1442	58.2
TOTAL	725	27.4	1360	55.3	394	16.4	2479	100.0

Table A5.2: Pooled Employment Equations Across Residential Location for Young White, Black, and Latino Males (assuming that educational coefficients' slopes are the same for each area, for racial/ethnic group)(standard errors in parentheses)

Variable	White Model 1	White Model 2	Black Model 1	Black Model 2	Latino Model 1	Latino Model 2
Constant	-.981**	-.990**	-1.318***	-1.307***	-.757*	-.749*
	(.352)	(.352)	(.203)	(.218)	(.444)	(.443)
Age	.077***	.077***	.094***	.094***	.061**	.059**
	(.021)	(.021)	(.012)	(.012)	(.026)	(.026)
High School Dropout	.080	.081	.033	.032	.266***	.276***
	(.066)	(.066)	(.036)	(.036)	(.078)	(.078)
High School Degree	.252***	.250***	.241***	.240***	.263***	.258***
	(.073)	(.073)	(.041)	(.040)	(.096)	(.096)
Child	-.069	-.066	-.062	-.067	-.005	.014
	(.070)	(.071)	(.051)	(.052)	(.106)	(.107)
FHH x Fam. Inc. ($0—$25,000)	-.397**	-.398***	-.082	-.087*	.111	.128
	(.163)	(.163)	(.052)	(.052)	(.245)	(.246)
TPH x Fam. Inc. ($0—$25,000)	-.131**	-.124**	-.180***	-.178***	-.071	-.077
	(.060)	(.060)	(.032)	(.032)	(.075)	(.075)
Family Income (>$75,000)	-.020	-.023	-.037	-.028	-.035	-.061
	(.049)	(.049)	(.040)	(.040)	(.090)	(.092)
Prince George's	.229***	—	.078**	—	.060	—
	(.057)		(.027)		(.067)	
PG Inner Beltway	—	.204***	—	.096***	—	.031
		(.063)		(.029)		(.071)
PG Outer Beltway	—	.249***	—	.024	—	.155
		(.061)		(.040)		(.102)
Adj. R²	.210	.211	.205	.207	.152	.158
Standard Error	.445	.445	.438	.438	.470	.469
N	725	725	1,360	1,360	394	394

References

Acs, Gregory, and Sheldon Danziger. 1990. Educational attainment, industrial structure, and male earnings, 1973–1987, Mimeo, Urban Institute, Washington, DC, October.

Acs, Gregory, and Douglas Wissoker. 1991. The impact of local labor markets on the employment patterns of young inner-city Males, Mimeo, The Urban Institute, Washington, DC.Allison, Paul D. 1984. *Event History Analysis*. Beverly Hills, CA: Sage Publications.

Anderson, Elijah. 1980. Some observations on black youth unemployment. In Bernard Anderson and Isabel Sawhill (editors). *Youth Employment and Public Policy*. Englewood Cliffs, NJ: Prentice-Hall, pp. 37–46.

Badgett, M. V. Lee. 1994. Rising black unemployment: Changes in job stability or in employability? *The Review of Black Political Economy*, 22 (3), 55–75.

Ballen, John, and Richard B. Freeman. 1986. Transitions between employment and nonemployment. In Richard B. Freeman and Harry J. Holzer (editors). *The Black Youth Employment Crisis*. Chicago: University of Chicago Press, pp. 75–112.

Barrett, N., and R. Morgenstern. 1974. Why do blacks and women have high unemployment rates? *Journal of Human Resources*, 4, 452–464.

Bassi, Laurie J., and Orley Ashenfelter. 1986. The direct effects of job creation and training programs on low skilled workers. In S. Danziger and D. H. Weinberg (editors). *Fighting Poverty*. Cambridge, MA: Harvard University Press, pp. 133–151.

Bates, Timothy. 1993. *Banking on Black Enterprise: The Potential of Emerging Firms for Revitalizing Urban Economics*. Washington, DC: Joint Center for Political and Economic Studies.

Becker, Gary S. 1957. *The Economics of Discrimination*. Chicago, IL: The University of Chicago Press.

Bendick, Marc, Jr., Charles W. Jackson, and Victor A. Reinoso. 1994. Measuring employment discrimination through controlled experiments, *Review of Black Political Economy*, 23, 25–48.

Berndt, Ernest. 1991. *The Practice of Econometrics: Classic and Contemporary*. Reading, MA: Addison-Wesly Publications.

Betsey, Charles L., Robinson G. Hollister, Jr., and Mary R. Papageorgiou. 1985. *Youth Employment and Training Programs: The YEDPA Years*. Washington, DC: National Academy Press.

Blackley, Paul R. 1990. Spatial mismatch in urban labor markets: Evidence from large U.S. metropolitan areas, *Social Science Quarterly*, 71 (1), 39–52.

Blinder, Alan. 1973. Wage discrimination: Reduced form and structural estimates, *Journal of Human Resources*, 8, 436–455.

Bluestone, Barry, Mary Huff Stevenson, and Chris Tilly. 1992. *An Assessment of the Impact of "Deindustrialization" and Spatial Mismatch on the Labor Market Outcomes of Young White, Black, and Latino Men and Women Who Have Limited Schooling*. Boston, MA: John W. McCormack Institute of Public Affairs, Univ. of Massachusetts.

Bluestone, Barry, Mary Huff Stevenson, and Chris Tilly. 1994. *Public Policy Alternatives for Dealing with the Labor Market Problems of Central City Young Adults: Implications from Current Labor Market Research*. Boston, MA: John W. McCormack Institute of Public Affairs, Univ. of Massachusetts.

Boston, Thomas D. 1988. *Race, Class, and Conservatism*. Boston, MA: Unwin Hyman, Inc.

Bound, John, and Richard B. Freeman. 1992. What went wrong? The erosion of relative earnings and employment among young black men in the 1980s, *Quarterly Journal of Economics*, 107 (1), 201–32.

Bound, John, David A. Jaeger, and Regina M. Baker. 1995. Problems with instrumental variables estimation when the correlation between the instruments and the endogenous explanatory variable is weak, *Journal of the American Statistical Association*, 90 (43), 443–460.

Bound, John, and George Johnson. 1992. Changes in the structure of wages during the 1980s: An evaluation of alternative explanations, *American Economic Review*, 52 (2), 371–393.

References

Bound, John, and Harry J. Holzer. 1993. Industrial shifts, skills levels, and the labor market for white and black males, *Review of Economics and Statistics*, 75 (3), 387–396.

Cain, Glen G. 1986. The economic analysis of labor market discrimination: A survey. In O. Ashenfelter and R. Layard (editors). *Handbook of Labor Economics, Vol. 1*. New York, NY: Elsevier Science Publication.

Cain, Glen G., and Ross Finnie. 1990. The black-white difference in youth employment: Evidence for demand-side factors, *Journal of Labor Economics*, 8, 364–395.

Cherry, Robert. 1988. Black youth employment problems. In Robert Cherry et al. (editors). *The Imperiled Economy, II*. New York, NY: Union for Radical Political Economics, pp. 121–132.

Cherry, Robert. 1989. *Discrimination*. Lexington, MA: Lexington Books.

Chew, Kenneth, and Felix I. Rodriguez. 1986. Urban industry and nonfamily households: 1970–1980. Paper presented at the annual meetings of the Population Association of America, San Francisco, April.

Christian, Patricia B. 1989. Nonfamily households and housing among young adults. In Frances K. Goldscheider and Calvin Goldscheider (editors). *Ethnicity and the New Family Economy*. Boulder, CO: Westview Press, pp. 57–73.

Clark, Kim, B. and Lawrence H. Summers. 1979. Labor market dynamics and unemployment: A reconsideration, *Brookings Papers on Economic Activity*, 13–60.

Clark, Kim, B. and Lawrence H. Summers. 1982. The dynamics of youth unemployment. In Richard B. Freeman and David A. Wise (editors). *The Youth Labor Market Problem: Its Nature, Causes, and Consequences*. Chicago, IL: University of Chicago Press, pp.199–234.

Clay, Phillip. 1979. The process of black suburbanization. *Urban Affairs Quarterly*, 14, 405–424.

Cole, R. E., and Deskins, D. R., Jr. 1988. Racial factors in site location and employment patterns of Japanese auto firms in America. *California Management Review*, 31 (1), 9–22.

Cotton, Jeremiah. 1993. A comparative analysis of the labor-market outcomes of Latinos, blacks, and whites in Boston, Massachusetts, and New England, 1983 to 1991. In Edwin Melendez and Miriam Uriarte (editors). *Latino Poverty and Economic Development in Massachusetts*. Amherst, MA: University of Massachusetts, Amherst Press, pp. 59–77.

Cox, David R., and D. Oakes. 1984. *Analysis of Survival Data*. New York, NY: Chapman Hall.

Culp, Jerome, and Bruce Dunson. 1986. Brothers of a different color: A preliminary look at employment treatment of white and black youth. In Richard Freeman and Harry J. Holzer (editors). *The Black Youth Employment Crisis*. Chicago: University of Chicago Press, pp. 233–260.

CQ Researcher. 1992. Youth apprenticeships: Can they improve the school-to-work transition? 2 (39), 905–928

Datcher-Loury, Linda, and Glenn Loury. 1986. The effects of attitudes and aspirations on the labor supply of young men. In Richard Freeman and Harry J. Holzer (editors). *The Black Youth Employment Crisis*. Chicago: University of Chicago Press, pp. 377–402.

DeFreitas, Gregory. 1985. Ethnic differentials in unemployment among Hispanic Americans. In George Borjas and Marta Tienda (editors). *Hispanics in the U.S. Economy*. New York, NY: Academic Press, pp. 127–157.

Dent, David J. 1992. The New Black Suburbs. *New York Times Magazine*, June 14, pp. 18–25.

Dowdall, George W. 1974. White gains from black subordination in 1960 and 1970, *Social Problems*, 22, 162–83.

Dunn, William. 1991. The rainbow comes to Prince George's County, *American Demographics*, Nov., 10–11.

Ellwood, David. 1986. The spatial mismatch hypothesis: Are there teenage jobs missing in the ghetto? In Richard Freeman and Harry J. Holzer (editors). *The Black Youth Employment Crises*. Chicago: University of Chicago Press, pp. 147–190.

Erickson, Rodney A., and Susan W. Friedman. 1991. Comparative dimensions of state enterprise zone policies. In Roy Green (editor). *Enterprise Zones: New Directions on Economic Development*. Newbury Park, CA: Sage Publication, pp. 136–154.

Farkas, George, D. Alton Smith, and Ernst W. Stromsdorfer. 1983. The youth entitlement demonstration: Subsidized employment with a schooling requirement, *Journal of Human Resources*, 4, 557–573.

Farley, John. 1987. Disproportionate black and Hispanic employment in U.S. metropolitan areas, *American Journal of Economics and Sociology*, 46 (2), 129–150.

Feldstein, Martin. 1973. *Lowering the Permanent Rate of Unemployment*. Study prepared for the Joint Economic Committee, 93rd Congressional Session, Government Printing Office.

References

Feldstein, Martin, and David Ellwood. 1982. Teenage unemployment: What is the problem? In Richard Freeman and David Wise (editors). *The Youth Labor Market Problem.* Chicago: University of Chicago Press, pp. 17–34

Ferguson, Ronald, and Randall Filer. 1986. Do better jobs make better workers? Absenteeism from work among inner-city black youth. In Richard Freeman and Harry J. Holzer (editors). *The Black Youth Employment Crisis.* Chicago: University of Chicago Press, pp. 261–298.

Fernandez, Roberto M. 1994. Race, space, and job accessibility: Evidence from a plant relocation. *Economic Geography,* 70 (4), 390–416.

Freeman, Richard B. 1982. Economic determinants of geographic and individual variation in the labor market position of young persons. In Richard B. Freeman and David Wise (editors). *The Youth Labor Market.* Chicago: University of Chicago Press, pp. 115–154.

Freeman, Richard B. 1989. *Discrimination and Poverty.* Cambridge: Harvard University Press, pp. 121–133.

Freeman, Richard B. 1991. The employment and earnings of disadvantaged male youths in a labor shortage economy. In Christopher Jencks and Paul E. Peterson (editors). *The Urban Underclass.* Washington, DC: Brookings Institution, pp. 103–21.

Freeman, Richard B., and David Wise. 1982. The youth labor market problem: Its nature, causes, and consequences. In Richard B. Freeman and David Wise (editors). *The Youth Labor Market Problem.* Chicago, IL: The University of Chicago Press, pp. 3–20.

Fix, Michael, and Raymond J. Struyk. 1993. *Clear and Convincing Evidence: Measurement of Discrimination in America.* Washington, DC: The Urban Institute Press.

Galster, George. 1987. Residential segregation and interracial economic disparities: A simultaneous-equations approach, *Journal of Urban Economics,* 21, 22–44.

Galster, George. 1991. Black suburbanization: Has it changed the relative location of races? *Urban Affairs Quarterly,* 26, 621–628.

Galster, George, and W. Mark Keeney. 1988. Race, residence, discrimination, and economic opportunities, *Urban Affairs Quarterly,* 24, 87–117.

Green, Rodney D. Green, and David M. James. 1993. Is job accessibility a serious problem for black workers? *Review of Radical Political Economy,* 23 (2), 85–92.

Green , Roy. ed. 1992. *Enterprise Zones: New Directions on Economic Development.* Newbury Park, CA: Sage Publications.

Greenstein, Robert. 1991. Universal and targeted approaches to relieving poverty: An alternative View. In Christopher Jencks and Paul E. Peterson (editors). *The Urban Underclass*. Washington, D.C.: Brookings Institution, pp. 437–459.

Harrison, Bennett. 1972. The Intrametropolitan distribution of minority economic welfare, *Journal of Regional Science*, 12, 23–43.

Harrison, Bennett. 1974. *Urban Economic Development: Suburbanization, Minority Opportunity, and the Condition of the Central City*. Washington, DC: Urban Institute.

Harrison, Bennett. 1977. Education and underemployment in the urban ghetto. In David Gordon (editor). *Problems of Political Economy: An Urban Perspective*. Lexington, MA: D.C. Heath, pp. 252–263.

Harrison, Bennett. 1994. *Building Bridges: Community Development Corporations and the World of Employment Training*. New York, NY: Ford Foundation.

Hausman, Jerry A. 1978. Specification tests in econometrics, *Econometrica*, 46 (6), 1251–1272.

Holzer, Harry J. 1986. Black youth nonemployment: Duration and job search. In Richard Freeman and Harry J. Holzer (editors). *The Black Youth Employment Crisis*. Chicago: The University of Chicago Press, pp. 23–70.

Holzer, Harry J. 1991. The spatial mismatch hypothesis: What has the evidence shown? *Urban Studies*, 28 (1), 105–122.

Holzer, Harry J., Keith R. Ihlanfeldt, and David L. Sjoquist. 1994. Work, search, and travel among white and black youth, *Journal of Urban Economics*, 35, 320–345.

Hungerford, Thomas L. 1994. Mismatches, isolation, and the duration of unemployment spells, Mimeo, U.S. General Accounting Office and the American University, October.

Ihlanfeldt, Keith R. 1992. *Job Accessibility and the Employment and School Enrollment of Teenagers*. Kalamazoo, MI: The W.E. Upjohn Institute for Employment Research.

Ihlanfeldt, Keith R. 1993. Intra-urban job accessibility and Hispanic youth employment rates, *Journal of Urban Economics*, 33, 254–271.

Ihlanfeldt, Keith R., and David L. Sjoquist. 1989. The impact of job decentralization on the economic welfare of central-city blacks, *Journal of Urban Economics*, 26, 110–130.

Ihlanfeldt, Keith R., and David L. Sjoquist. 1990. Job accessibility and racial differences in youth employment rates, *American Economic Review*, 80 (1), 267–276.

References

Ihlanfeldt, Keith R., and David L. Sjoquist. 1991a. The effect of job access on black and white youth employment: A cross-section analysis, *Urban Studies*, 28, 255–265.

Ihlanfeldt, Keith R., and David L. Sjoquist. 1991b. The role of space in determining the occupations of black and white workers, *Regional Science and Urban Economics*, 21, 295–315.

Jaynes, G.D., and R. W. Williams. 1989. *A Common Destiny: Blacks and American Society*. Washington, DC: National Academy Press, pp. 329–390.

Jencks, Christopher. 1992. *Rethinking Social Policy*. New York, NY: Harper Press, pp. 49–69.

Jencks, Christopher and Paul E. Peterson. 1991. *The Urban Underclass*. Washington, DC: The Brookings Institutions.

Jencks, Christopher and Susan E. Mayer. 1991. Residential segregation, job proximity, and black job opportunities. In Michael McGeary and Lawrence Lynn (editors). *Concentrated Urban Poverty in America*. Washington, DC: National Academy Press.

Johnston, William B., and Arnold E. Packer. 1987. *Workforce 2000: Work and Workers for the Twenty-first Century*. Indianapolis, IN: Hudson Institute.

Juhn, Chinhui. 1992. Decline of male labor market participation: The role of declining market opportunities, *Quarterly Journal of Economics*, 107 (1), 79–122.

Kain, John F. 1968. Housing segregation, Negro employment and metropolitan decentralization, *The Quarterly Journal of Economics*, 82, 175–97.

Kain, John F. 1985. Black suburbanization in the eighties: A new beginning or a false hope. In John M. Quigley and Daniel L. Rubinfeld (editors). *American Domestic Priorities: An Economic Appraisal*. Berkeley, CA: University of California Press, pp. 253–282.

Kain, John F. 1992. The spatial mismatch hypothesis: Three decades later, *Housing Policy Debate*, 3 (2), 371–460.

Kalbfleisch, John D., and Robert L. Prentice. 1980. *The Statistical Analysis of Failure Time Data*. New York, NY: Wiley Press.

Kasarda, John D. 1985. Urban change and minority opportunities. In Paul E. Peterson (editor). *The New Urban Reality*. Washington, DC.: The Brookings Institution, pp. 33–67.

Kasarda, John D. 1988. Jobs, migration, and emerging urban mismatches. In Michael G.H. McGeary and Lawrence E. Lynn (editors). *Urban Change and Poverty*. Washington, DC: National Academy Press.

Kasarda, John D. 1990a. City jobs and residents on a collision course: The urban underclass dilemma, *Economic Development Quarterly*, 4 (4), 19–31.
Kasarda, John D. 1990b. Structural factors affecting the location and timing of urban underclass growth, *Urban Geography*, 11 (3), 234–264.
Katz, Lawrence, and Kevin Murphy. 1992. Changes in relative wages, 1963–87: Supply and demand factors, *Quarterly Journal of Economics*, 107 (1), 35–78.
Kiefer, Nicholas M. 1988. Economic duration data and hazard functions, *Journal of Economic Literature*, 26, 646–679.
Kirshenman, Joleen, and Kathryn M. Neckerman. 1991. "We'd love to hire them, but...": The meaning of race for employers. In Christopher Jencks and Paul E. Peterson (editors). *The Urban Underclass*. Washington, DC: Brookings Institution, pp. 203–32.
Ladd, Helen, F. 1994. Spatially targeted economic development strategies: Do they work? *Cityscape: A Journal of Policy Development and Research*, 1 (1), 193–218.
Lancaster, Tony. 1979. Econometric methods for the duration of unemployment, *Econometrica*, 47 (4), 939–56.
Leonard, Jonathan S. 1986. Comments on: The spatial mismatch hypothesis: Are there teenage jobs missing in the ghetto. In Richard B. Freeman and Harry J. Holzer (editors). *The Black Youth Employment Crises*. Chicago, IL: University of Chicago Press, pp. 185–190.
Leonard, Jonathan S. 1987. The interaction of residential segregation and employment discrimination, *Journal of Urban Economics*, 21, 323–346.
Leonard, Jonathan S. 1990. The impact of affirmative action regulation and equal employment law on black employment, *Journal of Economic Perspectives*, 4, 311–334.
Lerman, Robert I. 1986. Do welfare programs affect the schooling and work patterns of young black men? In Richard B. Freeman and David Wise (editors). *The Black Youth Employment Crisis*. Chicago, IL: University of Chicago Press, pp. 403–438.
Lerman, Robert I., and Hillard Pouncy. 1990. The compelling case for youth apprenticeships, *The Public Interest*, Fall, 62–77.
Levy, Frank, and Richard Murnane. 1992. Earnings levels and earnings inequality: A Review of recent trends and proposed explanations, *Journal of Economic Literature*, 30 (3), 1333–1371.

References

Logan, John R., and Mark Schneider. 1984. Racial segregation and racial change in American suburbs, 1970–1980, *American Journal of Sociology*, 89, 874–888.

Lynch, Lisa M. 1989. The youth labor market in the eighties: Determinants of re-employment probabilities for young men and women, *Review of Economics and Statistics*, 37–45.

Massey, Douglas S. 1993. *American Apartheid: Segregation and the Making of the Underclass*. Cambridge, MA: Harvard University Press.

Massey, Douglas S., and Nancy A. Denton. 1988. Suburbanization and segregation in U.S. metropolitan areas, *American Journal of Sociology*, 94 (3), 592–626.

Mieszkowski, Peter, and Edwin S. Mills. 1993. The causes of metropolitan suburbanization, *Journal of Economic Perspectives*, 7 (3), 135–147.

Mishel, Lawrence, and Ruy Teixeira. 1991. *The Myth of the Coming Labor Shortage*. Washington, DC: Economic Policy Institute.

Moore, Thomas S. 1992. Racial differences in post-displacement joblessness, *Social Science Quarterly*, 73 (3), 674–89.

Mortenson, Dale T. 1970. Job search, the duration of unemployment, and the Phillips curve, *American Economic Review*, 60 (3), 847–862.

Moss, Philip, and Chris Tilly. 1993. "Soft" skills and race: An investigation of black men's employment problems, Paper presented at Eastern Economic Association Conference, Washington, DC, March.

Neckerman, Kathryn M., and Joleen Kirshenman. 1991. Hiring strategies, racial bias, and inner-city workers, *Social Problems*, 38 (4), 801–815.

Neidert, Lisa, and Marta Tienda. 1981. Converting education into earnings: Patterns among Hispanic origin men. In Marta Tienda (editor). *Hispanic Origin Workers in the U.S. Labor Market*. University of Wisconsin, Department of Rural Sociology, Final report to the U.S. Department of Labor, Employment and Training Administration.

Newman, Katherine S. 1995. Finding work in the inner city: How hard is it now, Mimeo, Department of Anthropology, Columbia University, New York, NY.

Oaxaca, R. 1973. Male-female wage differential in urban labor markets, *International Economic Review*, 14, 693–709.

O'Neill, June. 1990. The role of human capital in earnings differences between black and white men, *Journal of Economic Perspectives*, 4 (4), 25–45.

O'Regan, Katherine M., and John M. Quigley. 1991. Labor market access and labor market outcomes for urban youth, *Regional Science and Urban Economics*, 21, 277–293.

Osterman, Paul. 1980. *Getting Started: The Youth Labor Market.* Cambridge, MA: MIT Press.

Rosenbaum, James E., and Susan J. Popkin. 1991. Employment and earnings of low-income blacks who move to middle-class suburbs. In Christopher Jencks and Paul E. Peterson (editors). *The Urban Underclass.* Washington, DC: The Brookings Institutions, pp. 342–356.

Santos, Richard. 1985. *Hispanic Youth: Emerging Workers.* New York, NY: Praeger Publishers.

Sawhill, Isabel V. 1989. Rethinking employment policy. In D. Lee Bawden and Felicity Skidmore (editors). *Rethinking Employment Policy.* Washington, DC: Urban Institute Press, pp. 9–29.

Schneider, Mark, and Thomas Phelan. 1993. Black suburbanization in the 1980s, *Demography,* 30 (2), 269–279.

Shulman, Steven. 1990. Racial inequality and white employment: An interpretation and test of the bargaining power hypothesis, *The Review of Black Political Economy,* 18, 5–20.

Skocpol, Theda. 1991. Targeting within universalism: Politically viable policies to combat poverty in the United States. In Christopher Jencks and Paul E. Peterson (editors). *The Urban Underclass.* Washington, DC: Brookings Institution, pp. 411–436.

Sowell, Thomas. 1990. *Preferential Policies: An International Perspective.* New York, NY: Quill.

Stahura, John M. 1989. Rapid black suburbanization of the 1970s: Some policy considerations, *Policy Studies Journal,* 18 (2), 279–291.

Stephenson Jr., Stanley P. 1985. Labor market turnover and joblessness for Hispanic youth. In George J. Borjas and Marta Tienda (editors). *Hispanics in the U.S. Economy.* New York, NY: Academic Press, pp. 193–216.

Stoll, Michael A. 1993. Teaching trades: A pending plan to train America's youth," *Dollars and Sense,* November/December, 23–26.

Straszheim, Mahlon R. 1980. Discrimination and the spatial characteristics of the urban labor market for black workers, *Journal of Urban Economics,* 7, 119–140.

Stocker, Thomas M. 1986. Consistent estimation of scaled coefficients, *Econometrica,* 54, 1461–1481.

Suits, D., and R. Morgenstern. 1967. Duration as a dimension of unemployment, Paper presented at the Econometric Society Annual Meetings, New York, NY.

Thurow, Lester. 1976. *Generating Inequality.* New York, NY: Basic Books.

Tienda, Marta, 1994. Latinos and the American pie: Research and policy issues for the 21st century, Mimeo, Social Science Research Council, New York, NY.

Tilly, Chris, and Philip Moss. 1991. Why black men are doing worse in the labor market, Science Research Council, Subcommittee on Joblessness and the Underclass, New York, NY.

Tuma, Nancy B. 1989. Event history analysis: An introduction, Mimeo, Department of Sociology, Stanford University, Stanford, CA.

Turner, Margery Austin, Raymond J. Struyk, and John Yinger. 1991. *Opportunities Denied, Opportunities Diminished: Racial Discrimination in Hiring*. Washington, DC: The Urban Institute Press.

U.S. Bureau of the Census. 1973. *1970 Census of the Population*. vol. 1 Characteristics of the Population. Chap. C General Social and Economic Characteristics. Washington, DC: U.S. Dept. of Commerce, Bureau of the Census.

U.S. Bureau of the Census. 1983. *1980 Census of the Population*. vol. 1 Characteristics of the Population. Chap. C General Social and Economic Characteristics. Washington, DC: U.S. Dept. of Commerce, Bureau of the Census.

U.S. Bureau of the Census. 1985. *1982 Census of Industries*. Geographic Area Series. Washington, DC: U.S. Dept. of Commerce, Bureau of the Census.

U.S. Bureau of the Census. 1993. *1990 County Business Patterns*. Maryland and the District of Columbia. Washington, DC: U.S. Dept. of Commerce, Bureau of the Census.

U.S. Bureau of the Census. 1994. *1990 Census of the Population*. vol. 1 Characteristics of the Population. Chap. C General Social and Economic Characteristics. Washington, DC: U.S. Dept. of Commerce, Bureau of the Census.

Vrooman, John and Stuart Greenfield. 1980. Are blacks making it in the suburbs? Some new evidence on intrametropolitan spatial segmentation, *Journal of Urban Economics*, 7, 155–167.

Whyte, W. H. 1988. *City: Rediscovering the Center*. New York, NY: Anchor Books.

Williams, Donald R. 1989. Job characteristics and the labor force participation behavior of black and white male youth, *Review of Black Political Economy*, 18, 5–25.

Wilson, William J. 1987. *The Truly Disadvantaged: The Inner City, the Underclass, and Public Policy*. Chicago: University of Chicago Press.

Wilson, William J. 1985. The urban underclass in advanced industrial society. In Paul E. Peterson (editor). *The New Urban Reality*. Washington, DC: The Brookings Institution, pp. 129–160.

Notes

1. In this study, I use the term 'minority' to refer to black and Latino youth. Somewhat more problematic, I also use the term race to refer to these groups. Although many would argue that Latinos do not constitute a race of people and rather some notion of an ethnicity, I use this term for simplicity in the discussions to refer to these groups. I do not claim any scientific validity in its use.

2. The case of youth represents an interesting test of the spatial mismatch hypothesis since racial differentials in employment are much larger for youth than adults, and since youth are more likely to be affected by such a mismatch because of their limited ability to commute in relation to adults (Ihlanfeldt, 1992).

3. I have restricted my study to males because employment levels among black males has deteriorated since 1970, while they have remained fairly constant, yet low for black females (see Table 1.1). The hypothesis suggests that a spatial mismatch has eroded the employment prospects for blacks both absolutely and relative to whites. Thus, if the spatial mismatch can in fact explain low levels of black employment, it would be more true in the case of black males.

4. The spatial mismatch as originally conceived seems to be more appropriate for the Northeastern and Midwestern parts of the United States. A regional analysis, however, was not possible with the NLSY because of an insufficient sample size.

5. It should be noted that the employment difficulties of 16–19 year olds of any race are more severe than those aged 20–24. Their employment-to-population ratios and unemployment rates are lower and higher, respectively, than their 20–24 year old counterparts. Nonetheless, within each of these age categories, the same racial patterns in employment outcomes exist.

6. The term "ghetto" is used here to describe poor, black central city neighborhoods.

7. Restricting the sample to youth as a method to minimize the endogeneity of job and residential location is more likely to be successful for teenagers and youth in their very early twenties, than young adults who are in their mid to late twenties.

8. The NLSY is an ongoing study of 12,686 young men and women who were aged 14 to 21 as of January 1, 1979. Youth have been interviewed annually since the first interview in 1979 about their education, jobs, military service, training programs, marriage, health, and attitudes, among other things. The NLSY workhistory file provides a distinct data file detailing, among other things, the weekly labor market histories of those individual youth interviewed in the main NLSY file. Thus, information is provided on the specific labor market state, i.e., unemployed, employed, or not-in-the-labor-force, of each individual for each week in the survey year. The response rate in 1985 was over 95% of the original sample.

9. The sample size of the data is shown in Table A2.1 in the appendix.

10. Clark and Summers (1979) have shown that there is little difference in the states of unemployed and not-in-the-labor-force. To provide another measure of "unemployment," I included the jobless rate measure throughout this chapter. Joblessness is defined as being either unemployed or out-of-the-labor-force. However, like Clark and Summers (1979), I include only those who are most attached to the labor force in the not-in-the-labor-force state. In the not-in-the-labor-force state, I selected those who are not keeping house, not sick, and not going to school.

11. One cannot tell from this data alone whether or not the unemployment spells end in employment. It is also true that they could end in withdrawal from the labor force. However, Table 3.6 shows that a majority of unemployment spells end in employment for young males in either residential area. Therefore, since the spells in table end in a relatively short period of time, it is likely that they ended in employment.

12. It should be noted that all jobless spells end in employment, since employment is the only other possible state when jobless.

13. Clark and Summers (1979) point out that to make this calculation one must assume a constant flow into unemployment during this year.

14. Approximately 55 percent of the sample live at home with at least one parent.

15. To conduct the analysis in this chapter, I merged three data sets: the 1985 NLSY main file (demographic and socioeconomic data) with geocode

data, the 1984 NLSY workhistory file (weekly labor market data), and a macro-variable file I created using data from the 1982 *US Census of Industries* and the 1980 and 1990 *US Census of Population*, which includes macro-variables measuring the characteristics of central cities and suburbs within SMSAs. First, I merged the macro-variable file with the NLSY main file by SMSA code. This procedure attached to each observation in the main file macro data measuring the characteristics of the central city or suburbs in which that particular person lived. Second, I merged this data set with the NLSY workhistory data file. This procedure attached weekly labor market history data during 1985 for each individual.

Using this merged data set, I arrayed the workhistory variable to estimate the spells of joblessness. After arraying the workhistory variables, I selected those young male adults who were jobless, i.e., either unemployed or not in the labor force, at the start of the 1984 interview and traced their workhistories that year. I selected those who were jobless because (1), research shows that there is little difference between being unemployed or not in the labor force for young people (Clark and Summers, 1979), and (2), because the sample size of those only unemployed at the start of the 1984 interview was too small to conduct the analysis. Those who were successful in finding employment, i.e., had a completed spell of joblessness, by the start of the 1985 interview received a value of 1 for the variable work and also a value for the variable duration indicating in which week the individual received the job. Thus, the variable, duration, measures the duration of joblessness. Those individuals who were unsuccessful in finding a job by the start of the 1985 interview, i.e., had an "uncompleted" spell of joblessness, were included in the analysis but were treated as censored. They received a value of 0 for the variable work and a value of 52 for variable duration. As I explained earlier in this chapter, a probability of exiting the state of joblessness is imputed on the censored cases. This probability is determined by the groups likelihood of leaving a jobless spell in the analysis. 76%, 61%, and 70% of the central city whites, blacks, and Latinos, respectively, and approximately 82%, 62%, and 79% of the suburban white, blacks, and Latinos, respectively, completed their spells of joblessness by the 1985 interview.

16. The description of the theoretical model and data extraction is provided in the appendix, Section 4.1.

17. This particular job decentralization variable was used because data from the 1982 *US Census of Industries* was the most recent data on job location within metropolitan areas. Farley (1987) also used this data and found significant negative effects on black and Latino male unemployment relative to

whites. Also, it is clear that large majority of young males in both the central city and suburbs work in manufacturing, retail trade, and service industries. See Table A3.2 in the appendix for the industrial distribution of these young males in both residential areas.

18. See the appendix, Table A4.1, for a list of SMSAs included in the analysis.

19. The positive coefficient for the job decentralization variable in the duration equation is interpreted as having a negative effect on employment, and hence, on labor market position. The relationship between length of duration and labor market position is not always clear since extending duration of unemployment in some circumstances could lead to higher wage employment. To verify whether length of duration corresponds to worse labor market position, I regressed young males' average wage from 1983–1985 on job decentralization and found negative signs on the coefficients, though they were generally statistically insignificant in each of the racially specific models.

20. The South Atlantic region had the greatest percentage of black suburbanites, while the New England region had the least. For a more detailed discussion on the patterns and dynamics of black suburbanization see Schneider and Phelan, 1993.

21. This data on the "beltway's" population was calculated and provided to me by Maryland-National Capital Park & Planning Commission, Research Division and is based on the 1990 *US Bureau of Census* (STF-1A).

22. Using the 1990 Public Use Micro data samples for Prince George's County, I calculated that the median family income for whites, blacks, and Latinos in the 'outer beltway' was $54,000, $52,000, and 46,940, respectively, while the median family income for whites, blacks, and Latinos in the 'inner beltway' was $40,000, $35,000, and $41,000, respectively, in 1990. Conversations with planners in the Maryland-National Capital Park and Planning commission also confirmed that the 'outer beltway' housed more wealthy residents than the 'inner beltway.'

23. Since there is no data available on business location within the county, I confirmed that most businesses are located and most job growth has occurred in the 'inner beltway' through conversations with planners in the Maryland-National Capital Park and Planning Commission, and from my own casual observations in Prince George's County.

24. Job import ratios are calculated by dividing the total jobs located in an area by the total employees who live in that area. It reflects the number of jobs per working resident in an area.

Notes

25. The *US Census County Business Patterns* does not include jobs in the public administration industry. Clearly, public administration jobs are a large industry in Washington, DC. Thus, in the total employees category, I did not include those who worked in the public administration industry. I did examine the number of public administration employees who live in DC or Prince George's. In 1990, 19.0 percent of each area's employed residents worked in this industry. However, since it can be safely assumed that more public administration jobs are to be found in DC as opposed to Prince George's, the effect of excluding public administration jobs and employees from this table is to underestimate DC's job import ratio and overestimate Prince George's. Nonetheless, it is unlikely that these changes would alter the trends found in Table 5.2 over time.

26. The sample size is shown in Table A5.1 in the appendix.

27. The employment rate is defined as the fraction of the non-institutional population that has a job.

28. Marriage may also affect the likelihood of having a job. Since only 2 male youth were married in the sample I did not include this variable.

29. Family income is net of youth's earnings.

30. I ran both OLS and logit regression methods for equations (5.1). Logit methods are appropriate for dichotomous dependent variables (Berndt 1991). However, Stoker (1986) has shown that ordinary least squares may be more appropriate in a broad variety of circumstances. Since there were no differences between the results of the two procedures, I only show the OLS results because they have a more direct interpretation.

31. Less than 15 percent of the sample moved to PG or DC from another area since 1985. However, the census has no information on whether people moved to these areas after 1985 and before 1990.

32. Table A5.2 in the appendix shows that a PG residential location is significantly related to young white and black, but not Latino, males' employment opportunities, as the spatial mismatch suggests. However, the magnitude of young whites' PG coefficient is nearly three times as that of young blacks, suggesting that young blacks ability to get jobs in the best of situations is compromised by differential treatment.

33. I also ran equation (5.1) with the natural log of family income. This variable was significant and positive in each model for both equations. However, in both models of equation (5.1) the magnitude of the natural log family income coefficient was much stronger for young black and Latino males. Nonetheless, the use of a natural log family income variable did not change any of the model's results.

34. Prince George's County is made up of seven PUMA groups, four of which make up the 'inner beltway' portion of the county and three of which make up the 'outer beltway' portion of the county. However, two of the four 'inner beltway' PUMA crosses over slightly into the 'outer beltway' portion. So, at best, these identifiers are crude, but do provide enough information to conduct the experiment.

35. In both models, I also included a dummy variable indicating whether or not the youth used private transportation to work, i.e., cars, motorcycles, or trucks, as opposed to public transportation. This variable was positive, highly significant, and had a coefficient of approximately .70 for each youth group in both models. Although the magnitude of the interacted residential location-education variables became smaller with the introduction of this variable, the residential location-education variables for the most part remained significant and young white males' coefficients on these variables remained larger than those of blacks and Latinos. 44, 21, and 28 percent of young whites, blacks, and Latinos, respectively, used private transportation to work. This suggests that part of the employment rate differences between whites and blacks, and whites and Latinos is attributable to whites having more access to private transportation. I did not report this variable, however, because of the simultaneity involved in using this variable in an employment equation. That is, although private transportation may increase one's access to work by reducing travel time, one can only buy a private motor vehicle if one has steady work. Thus, the fact that more whites have access to private transportation than blacks or Latinos may simply reflect whites' easier ability to get jobs. Any employment equation that uses private transportation as an explanatory variable, then, must control for its simultaneity.

36. In Table A5.2 in the appendix, Model 2, where the educational variables are not interacted with residence, the decomposition shows that in PGIB blacks have a .01 endowment advantage, but a .04 treatment disadvantage. In PGOB, blacks have a .09 endowment disadvantage, and a .03 treatment disadvantage.

37. In Table A5.2 in the appendix, Model 2, where the educational variables are not interacted with residence, the decomposition shows that in PGIB Latinos have a .02 endowment advantage, but a .07 treatment disadvantage. In PGOB, Latinos have a .09 endowment disadvantage, and a .01 treatment disadvantage.

38. For more detailed discussions on the statistical properties of hazard models see Kiefer (1988), Cox and Oakes (1984), and Kalbfleisch and Prentice (1980).

39. For a more detailed discussion of the Weibull hazard see Lancaster (1979).

Index

Acs, Gregory, 77
Affirmative action policies, 19–20
Age
  in duration models, 70–71
  effect on employment, 108
Antidiscrimination policies, 19, 144
Audit studies, 21

Bates, Timothy, 100
Bendick, Jr., Mark, 132
Blinder, Alan 120, 128
Bluestone, Barry, 43–44
Bridges-to-Opportunity Program, 150

Central cities
  concentration of jobs and people in, 66
Community Based Organizations (CBOs), 143, 147, 150
Community Development Corporations (CDCs), 143, 147, 150
Commuting
  time of, 31, 33
  distance of, 31

costs of, 136
and transportation, 33
Cotton, Jeremiah, 53

Decomposition
  of employment models, 120–127
Denton, Nancy, 96
Discrimination
  consumer, 14, 77, 87
  employee, 77,87
  employer, 75, 84, 87
  housing market, 5, 17
  pure, 18
  racial, 17
  statistical, 18, 87, 142, 143
  studies of, 17–22
Dowdall, George, 75–76
Duration models
  for central city, 73–80
  for suburbs, 80–86
  discrimination in, 75

Education
  in duration models, 70–71
  labor market outcomes by, 102–103

185

effect on employment, 108
policies, 146
Ellwood, David, 25, 33, 38–39, 63
Employer Income Tax Credit, 145
Employment
  models by race, 114–115
  racial differences in, 10–12
  unemployment spells ending in, 59
Endogeneity bias
  residential, 13, 24–25, 32, 37
Enterprise Zones, 145
Equal Employment Opportunity Commission (EEOC), 143

Family income
  effect on employment, 107
Family structure
  effect on employment, 108
Farley, John 29, 75–76
Fernandez, Roberto, 36
Fiscal policy, 145

Galster, George, 96–97
Gautreax Program. *See* residential mobility programs
Greenfield, Stuart, 22

Harrison, Bennett, 22, 43, 52, 63, 143
Hazard functions, 157–160
Headstart Program, 146
Hiring queue
  hypothesis of, 37
  in duration models, 88
Holzer, Harry J., 27, 30, 39, 81, 84
Housing market discrimination.
  See discrimination
Human capital

wage equations, 20

Ihlanfeldt, Keith R., 29, 37–38, 81, 84, 94, 96

Jencks, Christopher, 15, 44, 64
Job accessibility
  definition of, 31
  studies of, 31
Job Corps, 144–145
Job creation policies, 144–145
Job decentralization. *See* job suburbanization
Job import ratio
  in Prince George's County, Maryland, 99–100
  in Washington, DC, 99–100
Job suburbanization
  in duration models, 70–71
  studies of, 29
Joblessness
  male youth rate of, 45
  in duration models. *See* duration models
Jobless spells
  distribution of, 60
  proportion of, 55
Jobs
  in Prince George's County, Maryland, 99–100
  in Washington, DC, 99–100

Kain, John F., 14–15, 29, 36, 40, 65, 86, 96, 131–132
Kasarda, John, 4, 96
Kirshenman, Joleen, 90, 117, 130, 144

labor force

Index

in duration models, 70–71
labor market outcomes
  in Washington, DC, 101
  in Prince George's County,
    Maryland, 101
Ladd, Helen, 145
Leonard, Jonathan, 35, 38
Location decisions
  of firms, 31
Lynch, Lisa, 77, 79

Massey, Douglas, 96–97
Mayer, Susan, 15, 44, 64
Mills, Edwin, 24
Minority business
  in Prince George's County,
    Maryland, 100
Monetary policy, 145
Moore, Thomas, 53
Moss, Phil, 19, 89–90
Moving-to-Opportunity Program.
  See residential mobility
  programs

National Longitudinal Survey of
  Youth (NLSY), 9, 44, 69, 77,
  79
Neckerman, Katherine, 90, 117,
  130, 144
Neoclassical Economics, 18

Oaxaca, Ron, 120, 128
Office of Federal Contact
  Compliance (OFCC), 143
Ong, Paul, 32
Osterman, Paul, 37–38, 133
Outward Bound Program, 146

Perkins Vocational Education Act
  of 1997, 147
Place-based policies, 145
Population
  in duration models, 70–71
  in Prince George's County,
    Maryland, 97–98
  in Washington, DC, 97–98

Residential location
  studies of, 22
  effect on employment, 107
Residential mobility programs,
  149
Residential segregation, 5
Rosenbaum, James, 150

School-to-Work Opportunities Act
  of 1993, 147
Sheltered workplace hypothesis,
  133
Sjoquist, David, 29, 38
Social Security, 141
Soft skills, 89
Spatial mismatch hypothesis
  definition of, 4
Standard Metropolitan Statistical
  Area (SMSA), 45, 70, 77
Statistical discrimination. *See*
  discrimination
Suburban residential mobility
  programs. *See* residential
  mobility programs
Suburbanization
  of blacks, 95
Summers, Lawrence, 44, 50, 54,
  59

Taylor, Brian, 32

Targeted policies, 139
Thurow, Lester, 80, 88–89
Tienda, Marta, 44, 50, 54, 59
Tilly, Chris, 19, 89–90

Unemployment
  compensation, 69–70
  distribution of, 60
  duration of, 48, 68
  dynamic measures of, 46
  frequency of, 47, 68
  in duration models, 70–71, 78–79, 83
  incidence of, 47, 68
  male youth rate of, 45
  mean weeks of, 51
  proportion of 55, 57
  rate in duration models, 69–71, 77–78
  rates by race, 49, 68
  static measures of, 44
  turnover rate of, 50
Universal policies, 139
Urban underclass, 5, 6, 15
U.S. Census, 9, 100
  of industries, 69
U.S. Department of Education, 147
U.S. Department of Housing and Urban Development (HUD), 149–150
U.S. Department of Labor, 147

Vroman, John, 22

Wage credits, 145
Wage subsidies, 145
Wilson, William Julius, 4, 5, 15, 140
Wissoker, Douglas, 77

Youth apprenticeship programs, 147
Youth Demonstration Act of 1977, 144
Youth Incentive Enrollment Project, 144

Zax, Jeffrey, 35–36

For Product Safety Concerns and Information please contact our EU representative GPSR@taylorandfrancis.com
Taylor & Francis Verlag GmbH, Kaufingerstraße 24, 80331 München, Germany

www.ingramcontent.com/pod-product-compliance
Lightning Source LLC
Chambersburg PA
CBHW061829300426
44115CB00013B/2306